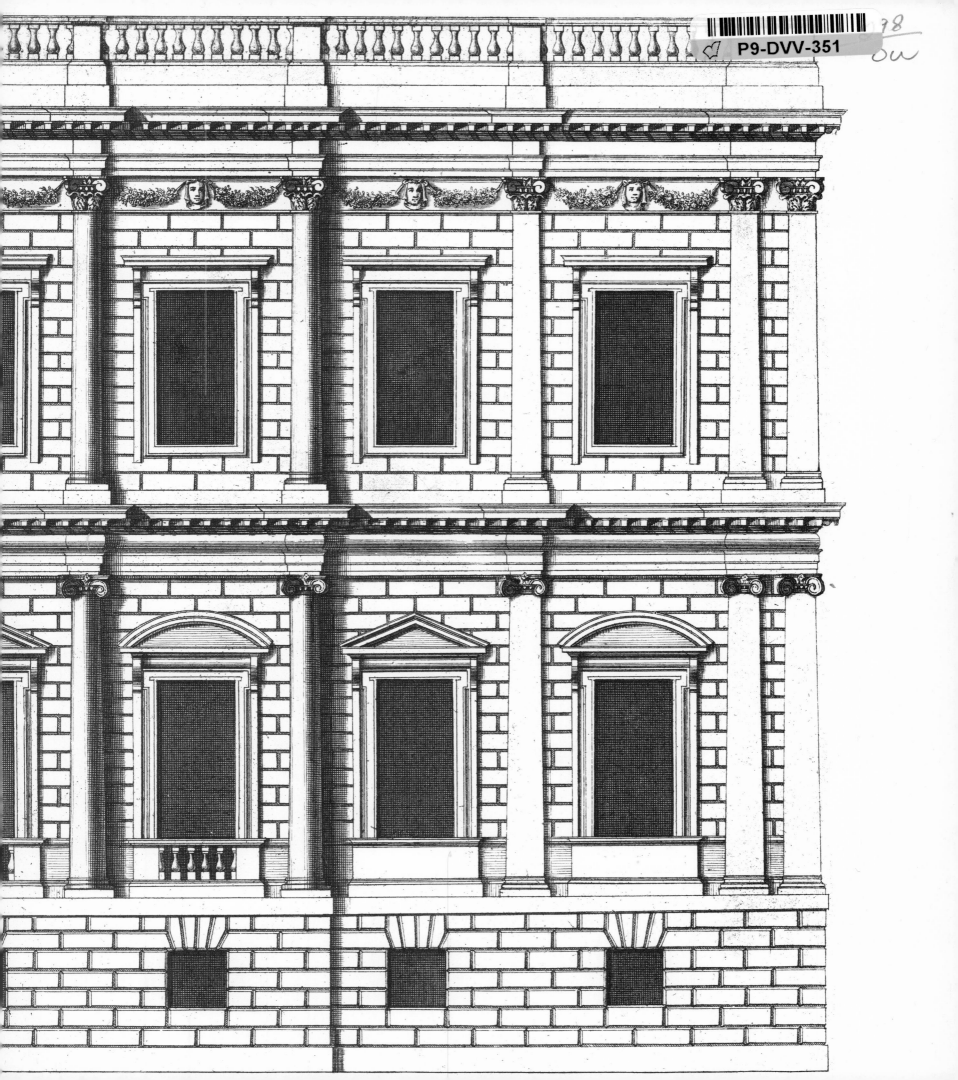

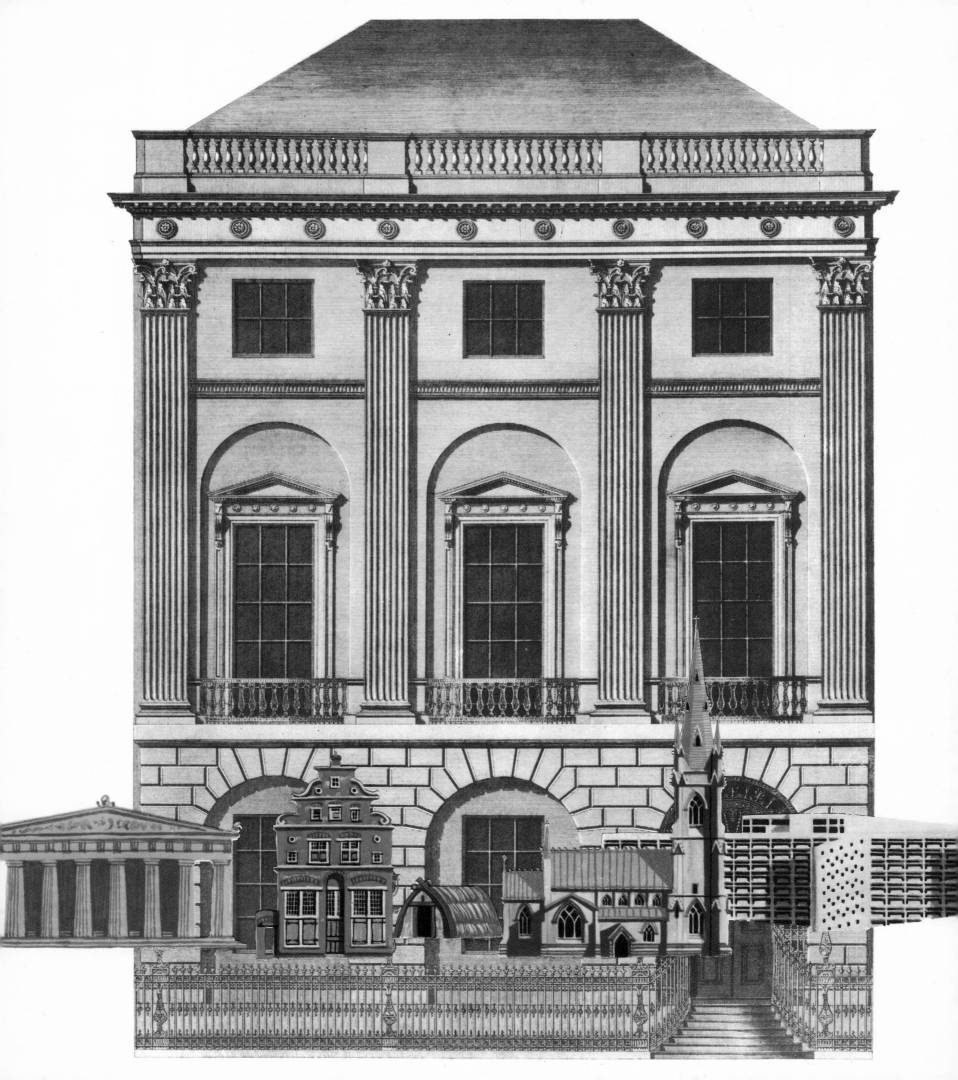

Learning With Colour
ARCHITECTURE
The Great Art of Building

by Trewin Copplestone

**Illustrations by Harry and Gwen Green
W. H. Stallion, Dougal MacDougal and Peter Warner**

Paul Hamlyn

London · New York · Sydney · Toronto

ACKNOWLEDGMENTS

For Sarah & Katie

Front endpaper: Detail from the Banqueting House Whitehall, London 1619 – 1622. Inigo Jones.
Back endpaper: Detail from the Secretariat Chandigarh, India 1952 – 56. Le Corbusier.

Published 1969 by the Hamlyn Publishing Group Ltd.
Hamlyn House • The Centre • Feltham • Middlesex
for Golden Pleasure Books Ltd.
© 1968 The Hamlyn Publishing Group Ltd.
Printed in Czechoslovakia by Polygrafia, Prague
T 1822

Photographs were provided by the following: A. C. L., Brussels 159; Aero – Pictorial, London 168; Alinari, Florence 18, 195; Alinari–Anderson, Florence 107, 182; John Amarantides, Arizona 223; Wayne Andrews, Detroit 211; Architectural Graphics, Connecticut 218; Bavaria Verlag, Munich 200; Bibliotheque Nationale, Paris 84, 205; Bildarchiv Foto Marburg 213; E. Boudot-Lamotte, Paris 10; Brecht-Einzig, London 82; British Constructional Steelwork Association 55, 56; Camera Press, London 28, 216; Cement & Concrete Association, London 229; Chatsworth Settlement 86; Trewin Copplestone, London 13, 100, 161, 191, 221, 228, 230; Lazzaro Donati, Florence 169; Farmers Weekly, London 4; Feature–Pix, London 188, 194, 209; Winslow Foot, Leeds 117; French Tourist Office, London 102, 150, 204, 219; Foto–Arnold 104; Ghizzoni, Como 88; Giraudon, Paris 20, 206; Librairie Hachette, Paris 126; Paul Hamlyn Archive 33, 97, 166, 174, 184; Hedrich–Blessing, Chicago 98; Michael Holford, London 65, 92, 94, 162, 192, 197, 198; D. Hughes-Gilbey, London 138; Institut de France 85; Alan Irvine, London 63, 64, 222, 226, 231, 233; Camilla Jessel, London 1; A. F. Kersting, London 14, 101, 105, 136, 139, 190, 208; R. Lakshmi, Delhi 95; Larousse, Paris 58; Leco Photo Service, New York 32; Mansell Collection, London 11; Mansell-Anderson 106; MAS, Barcelona 201; F. A. Mella, Milan 157, 183; Michael Norris, London 2, 5, 6, 12, 69, 70, 74, 76, 163, 165, 212; PAF International, London 41; Pictorial Parade, New York 215; Picturepoint, London 96, 103, 220; J. Th. Piek, The Hague 93; Josephine Powell, Rome 29; Peter Powell 54; Radio Times Hulton Picture Library, London 62, 202, 210; J. Arthur Rank, London 148; Rapho, Paris 9, 235; Constantine Reyes – Valerio, Mexico City 225; Scala, Florence 110, 111, 147A, 158, 173, 179, 196; Staatliche Museen zu Berlin 232; James Stirling, London 81, 83; Ezra Stoller, New York 217; Viewpoint Projects, London 135A; David Warner, London 7, 99, 164, 214, 227; Paul Watkins, London 34, 66, 137; Roger Wood, London 36; Z. F. A., Düsseldorf 203.

CONTENTS

chapter 1 ARCHITECTURE AND BUILDING 8

chapter 2 UTILITY AND CONSTRUCTION 12

chapter 3 DRAWINGS 32

chapter 4 DESIGN 38

chapter 5 BUILDING IN HISTORY 42

chapter 6 GREAT HISTORICAL STYLES 48

    Precivilised Buildings 48

    The Near East 50

    Classical Architecture 54

    Early Christian and Byzantine 62

    Medieval (Gothic) 64

    Renaissance 70

    Baroque 76

    Neo Classical and Romantic 80

    The Modern Period 84

chapter 7 DECORATION 88

    GLOSSARY 92

    INDEX 93

A NOTE TO BEGIN

This book is about houses, churches, schools, palaces and temples, theatres and castles, farms, garages and railway stations, airports, shops and offices. In a way it is also about dog kennels, cowsheds, pigsties and garden sheds. It may be about atomic power stations and car parks. It is about buildings of all kinds and all times in all places.

From the earliest times in history when people have lived in tribes or societies they have built, sometimes only primitive shelters, sometimes great constructions in massive blocks of stone, but always they have built. We are so accustomed to taking them as a necessary part of life, that most of us take them for granted. But they are, or may be, a fascinating subject for study and enjoyment. This book is designed to form an introduction to such a study.

The sort of building that people make shows a great deal about how they have lived and live now. Architecture is one of the greatest arts of any civilisation. Each great period in history has needed different types of buildings and each generation of people has thought differently about how they should be built and what they should look like.

In this book we shall discuss the kinds of buildings that have been erected, the people who have built them and designed them, the sort of training that they need, and what we mean by architecture and building. The first thing we must consider is the difference between architecture and building.

chapter 1 ARCHITECTURE AND BUILDING

What is the difference between building and architecture – if there is one? What, anyway, is a building – or architecture? It is important to have some idea about these two words and any difference that there may be between them, because through the book we shall have to use both words on almost every page.

This hut (1), if that is the word to describe the rickety structure, this garage (2), this dog kennel (3) or this cowshed (4) could be described as a building.

You would probably think it a mistake to call any of them architecture and you might think building was rather too dignified a word for them.

These houses (6) (7), this church (8), this lighthouse (9) or this warehouse (5) you would certainly call a building and most probably you would call it architecture.

If we look back at the illustrations we have seen, it is obvious that there is a great deal of difference between them all. That hut or shack, for instance, is just a pile of pieces of wood, corrugated iron, packing cases etc, put together to form some sort of a shelter. It is filthy and insanitary but is actually the home of a family of Chinese refugees on the island of Hong Kong. It performs exactly the same function as the Dutch house built in the 17th century. Both are homes for families.

The garage and the cowshed have some things in common but somehow the cowshed looks a better structure than the garage. Neither of them look as smart as the dog kennel. The church is different again and is perhaps more like the warehouse, than any of the other structures.

Which of these would we call buildings and which architecture and how do we decide? It is not always easy to decide which is what, and this book is partly about the difference between building and architecture.

Firstly, it would be reasonable to say that all architecture is a form of building but all building is not by any means architecture.

All the examples illustrated were buildings, even the dog kennel. A building can be any structure that is made to provide some sort of shelter, or to act as a container. It may shelter human beings or animals, it may contain anything from elephants to small insects. In this sense, the dog kennel is a building. However, we do not usually call such structures buildings when they are not designed or large enough for human use. Buildings are usually larger than the dog kennel. It would not then be usual to call a dog kennel a building. All the others – even, one must say, the Hong Kong shack – are buildings.

They are not all architecture, however. Probably no one would want to call the shack architecture. Why not? One dictionary

1

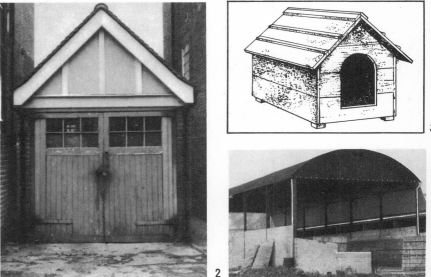

3

2

4

5

8

defines architecture as the 'art of building', not just building but the 'art' of building.

Unfortunately, this definition does not make everything as clear as might be wished since the word 'art' has proved to be extremely difficult to define. Everyone who has attempted it, artist or writer, has offered at least a slightly different definition from everyone else. There is some agreement about what it is about, but not exactly what it is. Most writers agree that it is to do with beauty and that this has something to do with rules, skill and intelligence. In architecture, as well as being concerned with the effective making of the building and its appearance, the art has also to do with the considerations of what the building is to be used for and how these things may best be provided.

This is all, of course, not defining 'art' but it is perhaps showing something of what it is about. Any building in which the architect (the person who is responsible for its design and building) has intended to incorporate these considerations can be architecture, and where he has not, it will not be architecture.

It might be helpful to consider architecture as intention and as

6

1. Hong Kong shack, housing refugee or squatter family.
2. Garage. Example of a utilitarian building made by mass production methods.
3. Dog kennel.
4. Barn. Example of a building found in all farming areas.
5. St. Katherine's Dock, London. 1824–8. Thomas Telford. Although warehouses, these buildings are extremely impressive and dignified architecture.

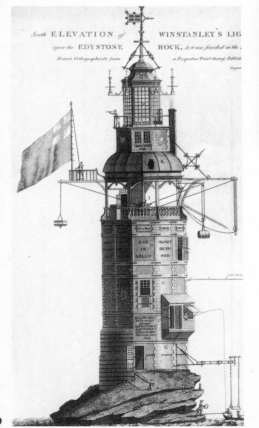

9

7

6. Château de La Treyne, Dordogne, France. 17th century. A large private house looking something like a castle.

7. House, Amsterdam, Holland. 17th century. Because of land shortage, these merchant houses in Amsterdam are unusually tall and thin.

8. Church of Notre-Dame-du-Haut, Ronchamp, France. 1950-5. Le Corbusier. Modern design for a church of unfamiliar form by one of the most important 20th century architects.

9. Lighthouse for Eddystone Rock, Devon. 1699. Henry Winstanley. Engraving by Thomas Smeaton.

8

expression; the intention on the part of the architect to give a building a form that he thinks is suitable and the ability to express this in the actual building. The quality of architecture comes from the quality of the architect's ability in both these aspects.

The ways in which he will be able to achieve the results he wants will be through the shape, size, proportion, siting and decoration and all these things must be considered by him.

This brings us back to that shack, or for that matter to the barn and garage. The shack just happened. The people who made it were desperate for some sort of roof, for something to shelter in. They had no money. They stole or found bits of wood and all the other things that make up their home and put them together as well as they could. It is certain that none of them stood in front of all the material they had collected before they started to build and said,

9

'I think the home should look like this' – nobody *could* have wanted it to look as it does.

But somebody certainly wanted the Dutch house and the chateau to look as they do. Le Corbusier certainly intended his church to look as it does. All these were made to look as they do because somebody actually wanted them to, because he felt that this was the best way to build this particular house. Another person might have done it differently, but for him it was right. The intention was there and the expression was there. The result was architecture.

Of course we must remember that there is good and bad architecture. Although we may not know exactly why, we do know that some houses, churches or schools are better than others.

What makes good and bad architecture are good or bad architects? Even though an architect may intend to produce a good house, he may not always succeed. It may be because he has not thought about it enough, or is not intelligent enough, or is not careful enough, or is just not original enough. There may be a number of reasons why he fails to produce good architecture but if his intention was there and he expressed it in a building, the building will be some kind of architecture.

In short, architecture does not just happen, it is intended. As we shall see later it may take all sorts of different forms.

If you now look back at the illustrations and at the ones on this page before going on to the next chapter, you will perhaps be able to decide which you think to be architecture and which merely building.

12

10

The illustration (10) requires some comment. It certainly looks as if it should be architecture. And it is. But the buildings are stables and we have suggested that the cowshed we saw earlier was not architecture. Is there some difference between horses and cows which makes a stable architecture and a cowshed not? Of course there is not. The stables here are architecture as the result of intention. The stables are the Royal Stables at Versailles Palace (11), built for Louis XIV, the King of France at the end of the 17th Century. They are part of the whole architectural idea of a palace which included stables with servants' living quarters over them. It is part of what is called the 'architectural complex', the group of buildings which makes up Versailles Palace.

This suggests that we should not think of architecture by the importance of the kind of building that we are considering. Architecturally, the Palace is not more important or better than the stables, just because it is a palace. A palace is not necessarily more important as a work of architecture than a small house, indeed there are many small houses that are finer than great palaces. Of course it is likely that the palace will be a more considered and careful work, and that it *will* be more important because usually there is more money, talent, and thought and ability engaged in building a palace than a small house.

In this chapter we have indicated something of the differences between architecture and building. We shall use both words throughout the book, 'building' as a general word to describe all the structures we are examining, 'architecture' when we are discussing the qualities of different buildings.

We shall finish this chapter with a quotation from Nikolaus Pevsner, an important architectural historian.

'A bicycle shed is a building; Lincoln Cathedral is a piece of architecture. Nearly everything that encloses space on a scale sufficient for human beings to move in is a building; the term architecture applies only to a building designed with a view to aesthetic appeal.'*

13

11

10. Versailles Palace, Versailles, near Paris, France. Late 17th century. Part of the stable block. Although a stable, this building is designed to be in keeping with the whole palace as shown in the engraving.

11. Versailles Palace, Versailles, near Paris, France. From 1661. Various architects, including Le Vau, J-H. Mansart and A-J Gabriel. Engraving, showing the palace before the chapel was built. The beginning of the park and gardens behind can be seen.

12. Tudor Houses, Lavenham, Suffolk. 15th century. Simple houses in an English town which look right in their setting and have been considered for their appearance.

13. Carpenter Centre for the Visual Arts, Harvard, Mass., U.S.A. 1963. Le Corbusier. A modern building where the unfamiliar appearance is carefully considered.

* *Outline of European Architecture by Nikolaus Pevsner. Penguin Books.*

chapter 2 UTILITY AND CONSTRUCTION

Buildings are made by people who have a special training. Nowadays, the people who design buildings are called architects. In the Middle Ages, they were called master masons (15). Whatever the name by which they are called, they have to deal with the same sorts of problems.

The first, and very often not the least, of these problems is the client. The client is the person or organisation, as for instance a government, who has asked the architect to design the building and has given him instructions about the kind of building that is wanted. We shall say more about the different kinds of clients later

in the book. At the moment, we shall assume that the architect has his 'commission' – that is, his instructions to start on the design.

Although the architect has in fact to think about all the aspects of this design at one and the same time, it will be useful here to divide them into two main groups, the practical and the aesthetic, and to consider them separately.

The aesthetic we shall consider later. The practical side of the design may again be divided into two parts, utility and construction. The first of these, utility, answers the question 'what?', the second answers the question 'how?'. What are the questions of utility that

14

15

14. View along the Nave, Westminster Abbey, London. From about 1000 A.D., extensions and alterations have been made to this abbey church so that it contains examples of all the changes in English medieval styles.

15. Building a cathedral. This artist's imaginative reconstruction shows how the building of a great cathedral was undertaken. If it is examined with care it will explain a great deal. Note, for instance, the unfinished pinnacle, the methods of transport for heavy stone, the scaffolding. The Master Mason in charge of the building can be seen in the foreground conferring with one of the clergy.

the architect has to answer? They are all concerned with 'what' the architect has to provide.

When he starts thinking about the building he is going to build, he has only the area of ground on which he is going to build. Nothing else. If he is building in a city, that area is likely to be very limited and enclosed on either side by other buildings. If he is building in the country, he may have so much space around him that he can put his building more or less where he wants. It was like this for the early people in history. When they wanted to build they did not have to buy land, they just had to find a place where no one else was living. It was like this for the early settlers in America (16). We can get a very good idea about utility if we think of the way they started. Heading west in a wagon, they stopped where they wished and said 'We will build our house here'. There was no one to stop them.

What did they do? They chose to build where there was shelter

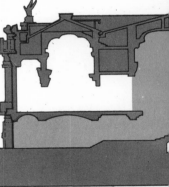

from weather, animals, and maybe from Indians. They had to be near water. They needed good grazing for cattle. In short, although they could build anywhere they wanted, they had to choose very carefully and consider as many needs and dangers as they could think of before they even started to build.

Then they had to think of what buildings they needed, a house to live in, other buildings for animals and storage. They had to think of what materials they would use and to choose a place where such materials, for instance stone and wood, were available.

When this had been decided they encountered the important architectural problem of space. Imagine them with miles of countryside, plentiful wood and stone, enough 'know-how' and labour to build what they wanted and all the time in the world to do it. How big *should* their buildings be, how much space should they provide in the buildings?

This is the architect's problem, how much space has he to provide? Architecture is a way of providing space. Walls, and roofs are only a means of enclosing space that is being provided. Architecture is, in one sense, the controlled provision of space. The architect has to decide what is the appropriate space for the needs of each building. His building has to have the right feeling of space for the use to which it is being put.

Those western settlers made themselves houses of the right size. Of course, they were limited by the materials they had, and their

16. Western log cabin settlement in the United States.

19 and 20. Opera House, Paris. 1861–74. Charles Garnier. The two illustrations show (19) side section, and (20) a view of the Grand Staircase. The coloured area in the section shows the auditorium and the area of the staircase is outlined by another colour. The staircase is nearly as large and more elaborate than the auditorium. Compare its relative scale with the Laurentian Library.

knowledge of building methods must usually have been somewhat elementary, but even so, they chose the space they needed within the limits of their abilities.

Not only has the architect to decide how much space to provide so that it is right for its use, but he also has to decide how he will relate different parts of a building, so that the different space needs in the building will be satisfactorily linked together.

When the architect has a number of rooms to put together, as in a private house, for practical reasons he may well decide to have all the ceilings the same height. But in certain instances – perhaps a palace or a hotel – he may need different heights of room. He has to decide how these will link together for effect.

Here is an example of a very unusual and original relationship

17 and **18.** Laurentian Library, San Lorenzo, Florence, Italy. 1524. Michelangelo. The three illustrations show (17) a side elevation, and a plan, and (18) a view from the entrance vestibule up the stairs to the long library room. There is a very unusual—perhaps curious—relationship of the vestibule to the library. The way that the architectural details are put together is also curious and may be called 'Mannerist' in style.

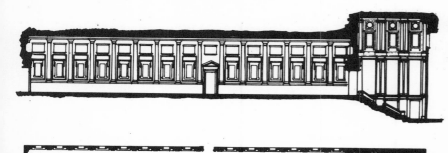

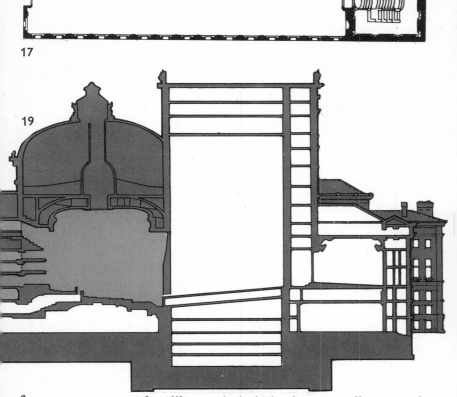

of an ante-room and a library (17) (18). A very tall, somewhat awkwardly tall, room which contains only a set of stairs leading up to a door high on one wall, is the ante-room to a very long low room which is the library. Here a deliberately unusual effect has been created. The ante-room is a confined staircase room leading up to an almost secret door – the door to knowledge and quiet meditation. The ante-room certainly invites you to climb the steps away from its own awkwardly tall shape – its tallness invites a movement upward. Inside the library, rows of seats stretching to the distance of the long, low and narrow room give a feeling of quiet and order, peaceful surroundings for study and is in strong contrast to the ante-room (regular divisions along its length suggest order).

Here is another ante-room with a different feeling (19) (20). It is, of course, not the same kind of building. This is the foyer of the Opera in Paris. Here magnificence and the promise of pleasure, theatricality and display are what is wanted. The great staircase sweeps around, corridors lead off, and arches and sculpture underline the feeling. It is the sort of place that would tend to make you feel important, happy, expectant, and a little awed – perhaps just the feeling that should precede going to the opera. In this cross-section which you can compare with the Laurentian Library, you can see how large and important the staircase hall is in comparison with the auditorium – the real reason for the building. In this building the ante-room is used for a different effect from the library and has, as a result, a very different form.

Modern architects, with new materials and the re-use of old materials in different ways, have different ideas about the space provision in buildings. The most obvious development is found in what is called open planning (21) (27). Open planning means that the space in a building is not restricted by the use of room-forming walls, which used to be necessary to support roofing but with new building methods are no longer essential, so that the interior of a building can be planned, starting from an almost entirely open space. Partitions may be used where they are wanted and shifted around when the needs of the building change. This provides a very different feeling from that of a room, a feeling of freedom and openness which can be carried to the outside of the building. As soon as a window is pierced into a wall a new feeling between the outside and the inside comes about. If a window looks out on to a wide valley with wooded and snow-topped mountains in the distance it

21. Interior view, House at Utrecht (Schroeder House), Holland. 1924. Gerrit Rietveld. This drawing shows one of the earliest open plan designs in modern architecture, by one of the important architects of the modern movement.

22 to 25. These four illustrations show how the size, shape and design of a window will affect the character of a room. The picture window on the right (25) gives a sense of open space which contrasts with the other examples.

21

22
23
24
25

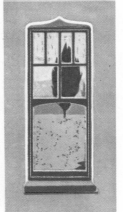

26
27

produces a very different effect from a window that opens out on to a blank brick wall. The rooms may be the same size but they will certainly feel different. If, instead of a window in a wall, there is a whole wall of glass the difference of feeling is magnified and the outside will seem perhaps more closely related to the inside (22–25).

There are other ways in which space may be considered. We have said that in the Laurentian Library or the Grand Staircase of the Opera in Paris the designers intended that there should be a definite feeling, and tried to produce it by their design. In both these examples the designers planned an effect that they decided was suitable. It may be possible to use the direction and containment of space with an even stronger and deeper emotional effect. It may make you feel fear or terror or awe or reverence.

In the Middle Ages, when the great cathedrals of Europe were being built, there existed a deep religious feeling that was so strong that it is seen in all the parts of these buildings. Their builders were very conscious of Heaven and Hell, the power and glory of God and the dangerous strength of the Devil. Their eyes were reminded of this all the time by the buildings. The view along the Nave of Westminster Abbey (14) shows how the space contained has a strong directional feeling towards the altar, the focus of worship, at the far end. The heavy columns are solid and enormous at the ground level but towards the roof they branch out like trees, become indistinct and almost seem to let the space, very enclosed at ground-level, flow out to Heaven. It is almost as if the only way out of the restricted life on earth is to move towards God and let your eyes look towards Heaven and Him.

It is not so much that the designers of these buildings thought in the way I have described. They would not have done so because the presence of God and the Devil was so real to them that they would not have been able to think about how they would express it. It would, I imagine, just have happened as a natural way of building a church or cathedral. Here space was used emotionally for a deep spiritual effect.

26 and **27.** In these two illustrations the difference in feeling between the traditional room interior and the open plan interior is shown.

28. St. Basil's Cathedral, Red Square, Moscow. 1555–60. Barma Yakovlov. This colourful building has nine campanile towers (bell towers), each with a different character and in different colours, in contrast to the Indian temple illustrated next to it, although both are religious buildings.

29. Muktesvara Temple, Bhuvanesvara, Orissa, India. 900 A.D. This form comes from the shape of the original reed shrine (as in illustration 38, page 22).

You will be able to think of other examples: palaces, for instance, or castles; temples of the East, such as the one from India (29) or Christian churches such as St Basil in Moscow (28) but these have a different form and have a different feeling.

The proper arrangement of space then, to some extent, *is* architecture. The way the architect or designer arranges the space in his building will show what sort of an architect or designer he is. The way he makes the space feel when you are in the building, and how that feeling comes from the form of the room or building, will give a very good idea of the success of this important part of the architect's design.

But whether the architect is successful or not in creating an appropriate feeling, he will still provide space – even a bad architect can make a big room or a small room. It is *where* to put *what* that is the decision he may not make correctly.

There is another important consideration that he has – circulation. Human beings, animals, and maybe machines, will have to move around in the building. Many things, from food to fuel, will have to be stored in the building. It will be the architect's job to think about the inhabitants' movements and where they will need their supplies of food and fuel.

Here is a building, Blenheim Palace (30), a large palace built by the British people as a present for the Duke of Marlborough. It is impressive because it is enormous and you might be tempted to think what a lucky person one would be to live in such a place. You could be right, but the kitchens and the dining room are about 100 yards apart. Food could and did get cold. In this building the creation of an impressive grandeur was more important than the simple convenience of the people who had to live there. Most architects who considered the convenient use of their building would put the kitchens as near as possible to the dining room.

The problem of movement is of course much simpler in a house than it is in any larger building that is used by the public. All sorts of extra problems are found here. Factories where different production processes mean many kinds of machinery give the architect very difficult problems of circulation to solve. One aspect of circulation is access – that is how the building is entered and how things are brought in and this involves the further question of siting.

The site is the area of ground that the architect has to build on. As has been said, he may have great freedom, like the Western settler, or the designer of a great country house set in its own lands, or he may have little choice with only a small area of ground. He may have no choice if he is replacing a previous building.

When the architect is considering where on his site he will put his building, he will have also to consider aspect. Aspect is the direction in which the building faces – north, south, east or west. Siting and aspect are together another important part of utility.

One of the most famous architectural sites in the world, the Acropolis of Athens, in Greece, is a brilliant example of the use of a magnificent site. This will be examined later in the section on Greek Architecture (p. 54-61).

What should be noted here is that considerations of weather, access, light, traffic will come into the question of siting.

There is one further utility that should be mentioned. It is the architect's responsibility to provide whatever services are needed in the building. Services are the facilities and necessities that may be brought into the building such as light, heat, water, sanitation and waste disposal (32). In most buildings these now include electricity, some form of piped water and complex drainage. It may include central heating and air conditioning. A number of other facilities may have to be arranged for, including fire extinguishers, lifts, escalators, laundry chutes, telephones.

These services may now be provided in one unit and form the core of the building as in this house by Buckminster Fuller (31).

The construction of buildings

At the same time as the architect is considering the utility of his building – what he has to provide and how this may be arranged – he has to be making up his mind about how it is going to be constructed. That is, how he is going to provide all that he decides the building requires.

In the past, the builder has had a limited variety of materials at his disposal, and has usually known only a few ways of constructing his building: in some parts of the world, only wood, in some, only stone of one kind, in some, stones of different kinds, in some, wood and stone. He did not know, in early times or in some parts of the world, how to make bricks or concrete, iron or steel. In this way he has been limited because all these materials must be used in different

31

30. Blenheim Palace, Woodstock, Oxfordshire. 1705–24. Sir John Vanbrugh. Perhaps the most impressive of the great English country houses, modelled on Versailles, it spreads across the countryside and displays the wealth, power and prestige of the Duke for whom it was built.

32. Service diagram. This section of an imaginary house shows just some of the provisions for the supply of services that an architect has to make.

31. Dymaxion House, prototype design. 1945. Buckminster Fuller. The components of the house would fit into the cylinder on the left and it was intended that the completed building should be transported in this way for

erection where required. All the services were supplied through the central core around which they were grouped. This design is an exceedingly interesting possibility for future house planning.

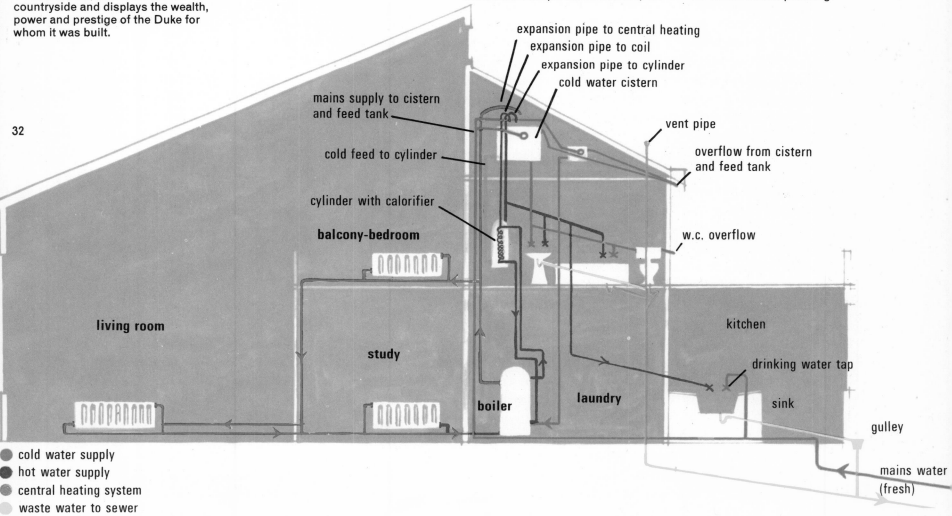

32

cold water supply
hot water supply
central heating system
waste water to sewer

ways – you cannot nail stones together. In early history, knowledge of methods of building was limited. For instance, none of the early people knew how to cover a large open area with a roof.

Now, it is different. Such a variety of materials are available and so many methods of constructing buildings are possible that buildings can now be of almost any shape and size required.

The modern architect will decide on his method of construction with various factors in mind.

Usually of course, one of the most important of these is cost. There is not a great deal need be said about cost here, except that some materials and some methods of construction are much cheaper and easier to use than others, and the architect must design in a way that he can afford. Of course, sometimes he miscalculates, and then building stops until more money can be found or he can save money on the design of other parts of the building. In the past, some buildings, like churches, were started without all the money needed in the hope that it would be found – and usually it was in the end.

The architect also has to consider the life of the building. By this we mean how long it will or is intended to last. In the past, people built without thinking of a limited 'life' for a building. They built as strongly as they knew how or could afford and with the most permanent materials that were available. There are a number of buildings from early periods in history still standing that show how successful they often were in this (33) (34). Most of these buildings have in fact outlived their usefulness and in modern times it has been realised that buildings should often be built with a calculated 'life'. This might be a long span of years or as little as a few months. Of course, the idea of temporary structures is not new. In the Middle Ages, for instance, most private houses were temporary wooden buildings, and even within the castles wooden structures were erected as temporary royal apartments. Around most great buildings in history temporary living accommodation was provided for the workers – huge barracks for the pyramid builders for example.

All these were built without thought of length of life, whereas now the use of the building and its 'life' are considered together.

Each method of construction, both of the past and the present, is particularly suited to certain kinds of building and it is the architect's choice of a suitable type of construction that makes a great difference to the success of his building.

When his knowledge of construction is limited, it is the way the architect uses the methods that he does know that determines the success of his building.

Although the method he uses is very important in deciding the shape and even size of his building, the method itself is not what makes a building well designed. More complicated methods are not better than simple ones just because they are more complicated, large buildings are not better than small ones just because they are bigger. Effective construction in architecture is the result of suitable materials used suitably.

What is meant by method of construction? As has been said, the architect has to provide shelter. Usually, this has meant walls and a roof for protection from weather and attack (animals, armies, or intruders) and to give a certain space.

Simple walls can be made by placing stones, one on top of the other, but unless the stones are carefully shaped so that they fit together it is only possible to make a low wall that looks more like a pile of stones, as in the illustration (37). Here are some examples of very early attempts at building (38) (39) (40) (41).

It was very difficult, if not impossible, to make an effective roof over these simple constructions and the early attempts at building were very rough indeed.

Almost all the energy of these early builders was spent on the structure and little consideration given to form and appearance.

Effective building began when stones were shaped so that they fitted together and it became possible to form a wall that could be raised to a sufficient height for men to stand upright. When this happened the invention of roof constructions became possible.

The early buildings used wood for their simpler constructions and wood was the first roofing material.

Long poles or beams were laid across the tops of walls and these were then covered with brushwood or animal hides.

From this developed the first architectural constructional method which is known as *trabeation* (33).

This is the post and lintel method. Either a wall or a vertical post supported each end of a horizontal piece (lintel). The illustration shows how this can be done (43).

33

34

Whilst wood was the first material used for both post and lintel, stone soon followed. The posts of stone were made of several pieces of stone placed one on another when a great height was wanted, but Stonehenge (41) shows how stone can be used in great single pieces. It also shows one of the difficulties of using stone for a lintel. Unlike wood, stone cannot be used to span a great distance unless it is extremely thick – it breaks too easily under its own weight if it is thin. The result is that a large number of supporting columns have to be used, which gives the inside of such buildings a forest look – as the inside of the Egyptian temple shows (42).

Trabeation in wood or stone has continued to be used throughout history as accompanying illustrations show.

One of the greatest limitations of this method of construction in either wood or stone, as we have seen, is that it cannot span really large open spaces in buildings.

The first of two early ways of overcoming this problem is the arch. The form of construction that comes from its use is known as *arcuation*.

This is a method of spanning a space between walls or columns with an arch made up of shaped stones (voussoirs) that fit together to give a semi-circular form (45).

This method requires more technical skill than trabeation. Each separate stone in the arch will tend to fall downwards and it is only the wedge shape that prevents this. Even so, the weight of each stone is pushing down and since it cannot fall straight down it causes what is known as outward thrust. This thrust tends to force the wall

33. Hypostyle Hall, Luxor Temple, Thebes, Egypt. 1408–1300 B.C. This view across the court shows the trabeational method. The bud capitals and the columns are fluted and they are surmounted by short, thick, slab lintels.

34. Montezuma's Castle, Verde Valley, U.S.A. 1100–1400. A cliff dwelling, primarily sited for defence, built by Pueblo Indians. Preserved as a museum, it has not been inhabited for several hundred years.

35. Egyptian capitals. Drawing. The capital is an important feature of an architectural style and two types illustrated here are the most typical Egyptian forms.

36. Hypostyle Hall, Temple of Ammon, Thebes, Egypt. 1530–323 B.C. The massive scale, the heavy blocks of stone, and the incised carving should be noted.

35

36

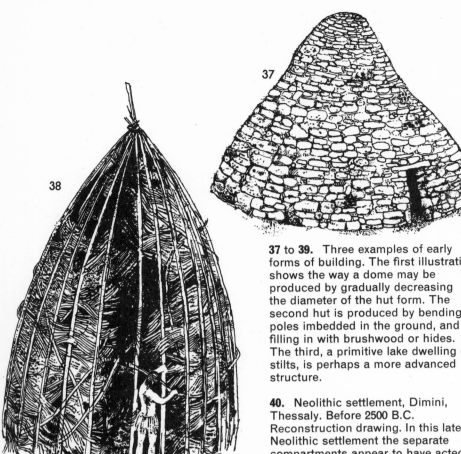

37 to 39. Three examples of early forms of building. The first illustration shows the way a dome may be produced by gradually decreasing the diameter of the hut form. The second hut is produced by bending poles imbedded in the ground, and filling in with brushwood or hides. The third, a primitive lake dwelling on stilts, is perhaps a more advanced structure.

40. Neolithic settlement, Dimini, Thessaly. Before 2500 B.C. Reconstruction drawing. In this late Neolithic settlement the separate compartments appear to have acted both as defence works and to distinguish living areas. The construction of the buildings is simple and usually takes the form of a lean-to shed. The walls are all of stone and the roofing is of beams and brushwood.

or column sideways from the top. The direction is down and out and the result is a line of thrust which is shown in the drawing (45).

To stop the arch falling in, all movement of the voussoirs must be prevented. This may be done in different ways. The building above and around the arch will prevent it from moving sideways (lateral thrust) at the arch itself, but the arch on a post or wall will need to be strengthened along the line of thrust. Usually this is done by means of a buttress. This is a heavy form placed against the post or wall strong enough to prevent the outward movement of the arch. It is found extensively in Gothic architecture.

Incidentally, if you look back at the trabeation diagram, you will see that there is no outward thrust. All the thrust is vertically down, and only the breaking of a lintel would cause outward thrust.

A building made with walls and an arch running along the length of the walls is said to be *vaulted*. The type of vault in this illustration is known as a barrel vault (46).

Similar to this vault is the dome (*domical* construction).

A dome is an arch in all directions so that if the building is cut through the middle in any direction it will look like an arch (a drawing showing a building cut through is known as a section). The part section drawing here is of the Pantheon in Rome built in 120

A. D. (47). In the Pantheon, the brick roof dome is made lighter through the use of what is known as coffering. Coffers are sunken panels used for reducing weight and for decoration. The dome of the Pantheon, being partly of brick and partly of concrete, is not a true dome, but even so the walls are very thick to counteract the outward thrust. Another remarkable dome, that of the Church of San Vitale at Ravenna (107-108) is made of pottery urns fitted into each other for lightness.

Domes of various forms of construction were used by early societies and were particularly attractive to the peoples of the East and Near East who showed great ingenuity in overcoming the technical difficulties of their construction.

The dome has also been used in the west. The Byzantine Church used it extensively and it was used in Europe for some of the great later churches, including St Peter's, Rome and St Paul's, London. In St Paul's a chain has been used around the base of the dome to help in holding it together.

The second of the early methods of roofing larger open spaces was the *truss*. This is somewhat similar to trabeation in that the truss rests on the top of walls or columns without any outward thrust. The truss is made up of separate parts, usually wood, which are

41

41. Stonehenge, near Salisbury, England. c.1500 B.C. This great circle of stones, placed in a series of two verticals and a horizontal crossing beam, illustrates one of the earliest structural methods of building. The groups of stones are known as triliths (*tri*-three; *lith*-stone). Stonehenge appears to have been a religious structure similar in building method to the Egyptian hypostyle hall.

42. Hypostyle Hall, Temple of Ammon, Karnak, Thebes. 1530–323 B.C. Reconstruction drawing.

40

42

fastened together to form one unit. There are different ways of making these units and each is given a name. Some examples with their names are illustrated (49). Wood was plentiful throughout Europe in the Middle Ages and wooden roof trusses were the most popular method for the great halls of castles and palaces. Not many have survived. Wood is not as durable as stone and catches fire easily – and in the Middle Ages, although fireplaces were used, domestic fires were frequently in the middle of the floor with sparks flying to the roof. Also, of course, the castles were under frequent attack. One of the greatest that still survives is the roof of Westminster Hall, London (51).

It was during the Middle Ages, too, that the great Christian cathedrals and churches of Europe were built and in these we see the development of *vaulting* (50). We have mentioned the barrel vault that comes from the arch, and during the Middle Ages the method of vaulting used earlier by the Romans was explored with astonishing results. The master-masons found that it was possible, by balancing the thrust with weight and buttress to achieve high and open interiors of a kind not seen before.

They started with round arches and later pointed arches were invented, which gave much more freedom of design. You will see examples later in the book which show some of the ways that stone was used in vaulting with almost incredible ease. The medieval builders were engineers of the highest ability.

Also, in the Middle Ages and later, another form of construction was widely used, which has been adapted to modern use. Here is what is known as a cruck house (52). The two beams that you can see at the end of the house are known as crucks and these are fastened together with a roof pole, as in the drawing, to provide a frame on which the structure is made. It is an early form of *frame* construction, and is like a roof truss used for the whole building. The Tudor house is a later and better known example of frame building, where the whole building is a framework which is filled in (53). You can see the framework in the illustration of an old barn which has been stripped for repair (54).

Early buildings were limited in size because of the strength and size of wood available. Stone is not suitable for frame construction.

When iron and steel came into use, it was possible to return to frame construction because these metals could be bolted or welded together to make large or small constructions. The great skyscrapers of New York were built in this way.

In all frame constructions the strength of the building lies in the frame, and the spaces between the frame can be filled in with less strong, lighter materials (55) (56). In the Tudor house brick, laths and plaster, or mud and wattle, were used. In the large modern frame structure, it may be any of the modern durable materials such as concrete, plastics, glass or metal.

The modern use of frame construction allows architects to make buildings which look very different from those of earlier times. With a frame, one part may be balanced against another so that the

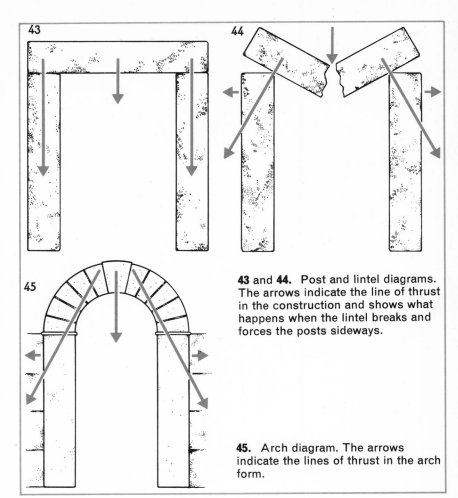

43 and **44.** Post and lintel diagrams. The arrows indicate the line of thrust in the construction and shows what happens when the lintel breaks and forces the posts sideways.

45. Arch diagram. The arrows indicate the lines of thrust in the arch form.

46

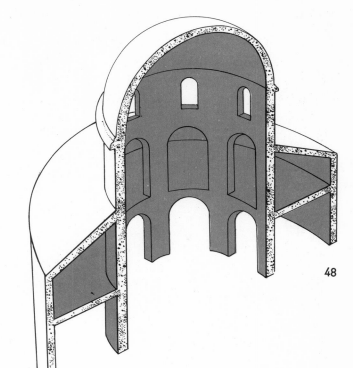

47

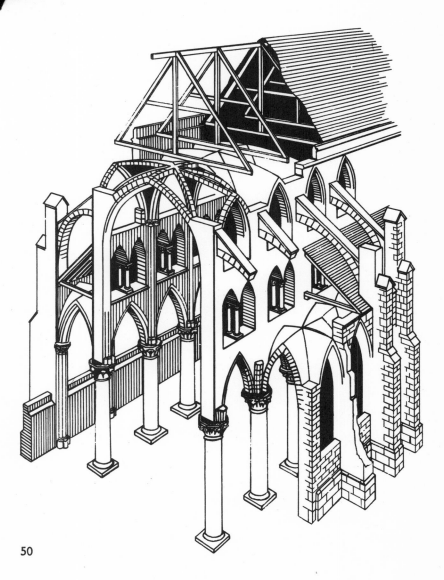

48

46. Priory Church, Payerne, Switzerland. c. 1040–1100 A.D. The view along the nave of this church shows a ribbed barrel vault. The clerestory windows over the aisle illuminate the interior.

47. The Pantheon, Rome. A.D. 120–4. This religious building is one of the great masterpieces of Roman architecture. It was until recently the largest single enclosed space, and the methods used to construct it are not fully known. The dome is of concrete and its weight is reduced by the use of coffers (sunken panels). As a single unit the dome acts more as a circular lintel than a dome, and so the outward thrust is minimised. Thus there are no buttresses on the outer walls.

48. Diagram of circular building showing use of dome. The outward thrust of the dome is carried out through the surrounding aisle.

49. Diagram examples of roof truss forms used in the Middle Ages:—
1. Tie-beam. 2. King post. 3. Tie-beam. King and Queen post. 4. Hammer-beam.

50. Cathedral or church construction diagram. This diagram shows how the more complicated problems of great church buildings are solved by buttresses and flying buttresses—an extension of the arch system.

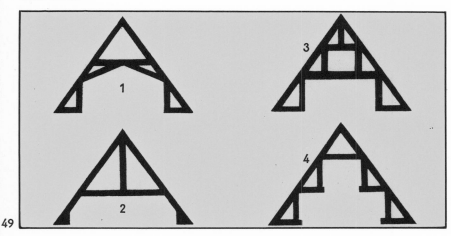

49

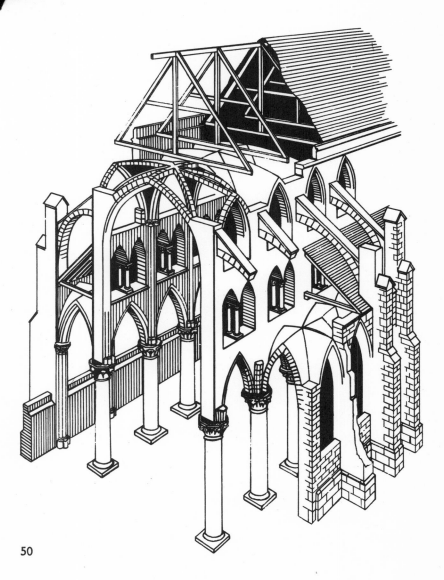

50

51

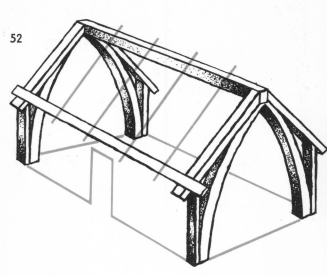

supports of the building may be very slender. The frame may allow the use of cantilevers (57). This is a system of construction where the frame is used to enable parts of the building to be free of the ground and even jut forward from it, the weight being balanced back into the building.

Another development in modern architecture is the use of *reinforced concrete*. This is a method which greatly increases the strength of concrete by embedding rods or meshes of steel in it during casting.

Although not in itself a method of construction, reinforced concrete is a material which has given the architect new opportunities for designing much freer shapes to his buildings, since its lightness and strength allows him to cover large open spaces without the use of walls. Nervi's Exhibition Hall in Turin (58) is a good example.

The materials of building

Until recently, the materials used for building varied very little through history. It is most interesting to realise, for instance, that the brick used in house building today is very similar to the brick used in houses built 4,000 years ago. The materials used were the most suitable, the closest at hand, and, of course, the shape and size of the building were greatly affected by what could be found. Where similar materials are found in different places there is often a sur-

prising similarity between the buildings. Houses found in Norfolk and Sussex show the similarity from different areas using flint as the building material (59) (60).

When large and important buildings have been required, like palaces or temples, and expense was no object, even in early societies, materials were brought long distances. Some of the temples of Egypt were built from red granite quarried high up the Nile at Aswan and shipped down the river to Lower Egypt in large blocks – an enormous undertaking at that time (see map of Nile).

In modern times of course it is different. With the methods of transport it is easier to carry materials, much modern building material is manufactured, building methods have become more standardised (that is, made to an agreed size or proportion of an agreed material), modern methods of manufacture have led to specialisation in particular building materials and all these things have diminished the importance of local building materials. Nevertheless the traditional materials continue to be used.

Each material has its own particular qualities and some of the more important are considered below.

Wood

This is the earliest and most extensively used material in building,

55

56

53. Tudor, timber frame construction. This illustration shows a typical Tudor wood frame building which has been opened to show how the structure depends on the frame and the walls are merely filled in with brick or wattle. It is the same method as the steel frame construction of the present day.

54. Barn under repair. When only the structural posts and beams are left the form of the building is still clear.

55 and **56.** These two illustrations show the same building in two stages of construction. The shape of the building is made in the steel frame (55) and the walls are made by adding precast panels (56).

54

as it was usually freely available locally. There are few buildings which do not contain some wood. Wood was used for construction in the first instance and continued to be used even when buildings were largely made of stone. For instance, roofs in early buildings were almost always of wood and even today the majority of roof structures in smaller houses are of wood. Go to any building being put up and you will see all sorts of different woods. In some parts of the world, like Scandinavia, wood is plentiful and is used for the construction of the whole building as in the Swiss chalet.

The great variety in quality of woods makes it a very useful building material. It can be very hard, as with teak or oak, or very soft so that it can be easily worked and carved. Woods are in fact usually divided into hardwoods and softwoods and each type has a place in building.

Unfortunately, it is also very open to damage by damp and attack by destructive elements such as woodworm. It is not really very long-lasting unless carefully maintained.

Another important quality of wood is that people generally find it an attractive material. It has a pleasant colour and is pleasant to touch. This is, of course, an important factor in its favour as a building material.

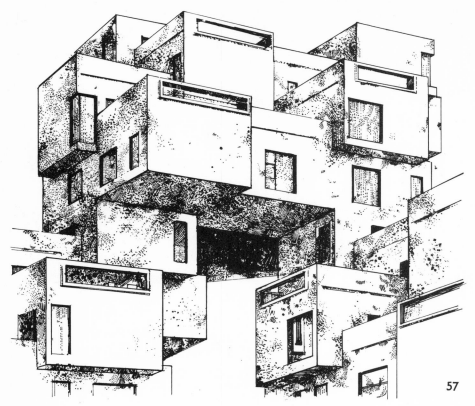

57 58

Stone

Like wood, stone has been, and continues to be, used everywhere in building. It is the most obvious building material, especially for larger buildings which are intended to be long-lasting. It is strong, durable and, unlike wood, it withstands the effect of weather very well. It can be shaped and carved exactly as wanted. Like wood, it is found in a variety of qualities and of colours and textures. It can be hard or soft – you cannot easily carve your initials in granite but you can in sandstone.

There are very few areas of the world where a suitable building stone cannot be found and quarried.

Brick

One area where suitable stone is not found is the land through which the rivers Tigris and Euphrates flow, known as Mesopotamia (see map page 48). The soil is thick mud and clay left by these big rivers and no trees grow on it. It was here, and from this soil, that the first bricks were made. These were rectangular in shape and were dried in the sun until they were solid and hard. They were frequently strengthened with small pieces of straw. These bricks were usually covered with an outer coating of thin, kiln or oven-baked bricks or decorated tiles which were more resistant to the heavy seasonal rains.

Since the time of the great empires of Assyria, Babylon, and Egypt, over 5,000 years ago, bricks have continued to be used. Sometimes they are sun-dried but more usually kiln-fired. The Greeks used them and so did the Romans throughout their Empire. Through the Romans, bricks came to be used extensively throughout Europe and are now one of the most common building

materials in the world.

Bricks vary in colour from white-cream to deep purple or black, but the most common colour is a reddish brown. The colour of brick is determined either by the kind of clay used or by the addition of colouring matter, and the range of colour has been of great value to the designer of buildings.

Bricks are used mainly for making walls. They are placed side by side, row upon row, and are bonded together with mortar. Mortar is usually a mixture of lime and sand, but it can be made of any materials that will hold the bricks together. In Mesopotamia, bitumen from local springs was used.

Bricks may be laid in different ways, known as bonds and patterns and each of these is known by a different bond name. In the illustration you will see some of the more common patterns (61). (Bricks placed end on are known as headers and those placed side on as stretchers.) Cavity walls, now the usual type, are those where two walls are made with a small airspace between the two parts being bonded by small metal bars (61). The value of such walls lie in their damp-resisting and insulating qualities.

Concrete

This is a mixture of sand, lime, pebbles or broken stones which hardens into a solid mass of great strength. This hardening takes some time and before it occurs the concrete is like a thick mud which can be poured where it is required.

Moulds are made to receive the wet concrete. For buildings, these are usually made of wooden planks fastened together and are known as shuttering.

The concrete was always in the past covered with a finishing

57. Prefabricated flats, Montreal, Canada. 1966–7. Moshe Safdie. Each flat is made as a concrete unit and they are all assembled together like a jigsaw on the site. They are assembled irregularly and provide different and exciting views from every angle—almost like a sculpture made of houses.

58. Palazzo del Lavoro, Turin, 1961. Pier Luigi Nervi. These reinforced concrete columns and ribs, designed by the greatest exponent of reinforced concrete, show how a design based on structural shapes can be attractive to look at.

59 and **60.** Examples of two buildings using flint, one in Norfolk (59), and one in Sussex (60). The similarity comes out of the qualities of the material.

61. Methods of laying bricks. Bricks may be put together to form a wall in a number of different patterns, depending on whether they are laid end or longways. The two most common methods are known as English and Flemish bond. (Bricks placed with their ends forming the wall face are known as headers; those with their sides forming the wall face as stretchers). A course is a layer of brick in a wall. English Bond is formed by alternate courses of headers and stretchers. Flemish Bond is formed by alternate headers and stretchers in each course. Cavity walls are formed by two, parallel wall faces with a small space between, making one wall.

material like marble. This is a veneer, rather like the veneer which is frequently found on various pieces of furniture.

Concrete will harden even under water and it is therefore very fine material for all climates. It has been used in one form or another since the Romans, who used it extensively.

Nowadays, it is used with metal as reinforced concrete and is becoming one of the most widely used of all modern building materials, since it can be used in a great variety of ways and has great tensile and compressive strength. (The mild steel has the tensile strength and the concrete the compressive strength) (63) (64) (66).

Metal

Ever since their discovery, metals have been used in some way as building materials, in early civilisations mainly in minor ways such as cleats or brackets. Most metals require very careful treatment against the effects of air and weather. For instance, iron and aluminium oxidise and their use as a building material is therefore limited unless specially treated in ways sometimes only recently discovered. The cost in producing metals in the sizes and quantities needed for buildings have also limited its use in the past.

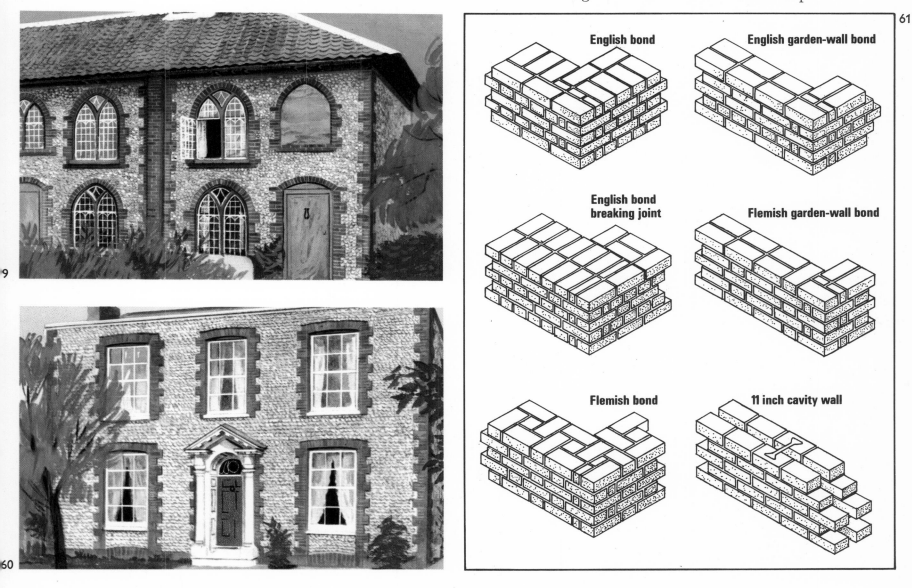

61

English bond

English garden-wall bond

English bond breaking joint

Flemish garden-wall bond

Flemish bond

11 inch cavity wall

It was only with the Industrial Revolution starting in the 18th century that iron and steel came into extensive use in building. The Great Exhibition building of 1851 in cast iron and glass showed what could be done (62).

The use of steel in frame construction and the development of new metals suggest that metals are likely to become more and more important in building in the future.

Here are one or two examples of the unusual use of metal in building.

Glass

There are, of course, other materials which are used non-structurally in building. Perhaps the most important and widely used of these is glass.

Glass is of very ancient origin; it was certainly known to the Egyptians and they used it for beads and other decorations. Its use in architecture dates from the Romans, who used it for windows. It has been found during the excavations of Pompeii, which was buried by the eruption of Vesuvius in 89 A.D.

Since then, most important buildings contained some window glass. During the Middle Ages, when the great cathedrals were built, coloured glass was used in the large, richly-patterned windows to illustrate the story of Christianity (65). These windows are regarded as a beautiful and important part of the over-all architectural design.

Toughened glass, like bullet-proof glass, will stand up to so much hard wear and rough treatment that it can be used for other purposes than windows such as walls, infill panels, doors and other interior fittings. Its use as a structural material seems likely in the future.

Plastics

In the last few years, there has been an enormous increase in the production of a great variety of plastics. Toys, furniture, tools, boxes and packages are all now made in plastic. All these are manufactured materials and with the technical knowledge that is now available, it is possible to produce plastic materials that will meet all our demands, hard or soft, brittle or flexible, in any colour.

The architect can now order plastic materials which will be as strong as he wants. What is also important is that plastics can be cast in any required shape. It is as easy to cast a window as a model car. It is obvious that plastics will be used more and more in architecture in the future.

All the new materials that have become available from plastics to treated metals have given the architect new opportunities for design. Because they have different properties they may enable the architect to use different methods of construction that were just not possible before.

As a result, entirely new forms and exciting ideas are being tried in building. Some of them are certain to be prototypes for the houses, shops, offices and factories of the future.

62. Crystal Palace, London. 1850–1. Sir Joseph Paxton. Drawn illustration. This vast, iron and glass construction housed the Great Exhibition held in London in 1851. Based on a design for a large greenhouse, built for the Duke of Devonshire at Chatsworth, the Crystal Palace was built in only nine months, through the use of pre-cast iron units.

63   64

63 and **64.** Tokyo Cathedral, Japan. Kenzo Tange. This extraordinarily imaginative and impressive building shows the use of reinforced concrete to produce parabolic curves. The interior illustration also shows the effect of the wooden shuttering on the surface of the cast concrete.

65. Canterbury Cathedral. Stained glass window. 13th century. Stained glass was used throughout the Middle Ages, as both a form of decorative story-telling and a means of illuminating church interiors with a controlled light and colour.

66. Marina City Chicago, Twin Towers. Finished 1966, Bertrand Goldberg. These Twin Towers contained flats on the upper 40 floors, garage space in the lower 19 floors, the core of the Towers providing all-service facilities; at ground floor level there are boat anchorage swimming pool, skating rink, theatre, and the whole complex includes a 16 storey office block.

chapter 3 DRAWINGS

You may not have seen an architect's 'working drawing'. It is called a working drawing because from it the builder can read the information that he needs to complete his part of the building – that is, he can work from it. It is complicated and requires knowledge and experience to understand. Nevertheless, it is the best way that the architect can explain to all the different people who have to work on the building, from plumbers to painters, what he wants them to know (67-68).

The architect uses drawings to explain what he wants done, and how it is to be done, in the way most people use letters or reports or even books. Of course, he has to write letters and reports – a great number of letters and long reports – but when he is explaining what is to be done in the actual building he nearly always uses drawings.

Drawings are much the best way he has of explaining a building. Although buildings are three-dimensional (that is, not flat) drawings can be used to express this very well – more precisely usually, than a three-dimensional model.

There are a number of different kinds of drawings that the architect can use, depending on the information that he wants to convey. The most important of these are:

Plans

Here is a photograph of a very simple shape (69). It might be a simple building. A plan is what it would look like from above. A plan can be made of any building or any part of a building, at any level in the building. Here, for instance, is the same building cut across the middle and here is a plan at that level (70—71). Illustrations (72) and (73) show the plan from above.

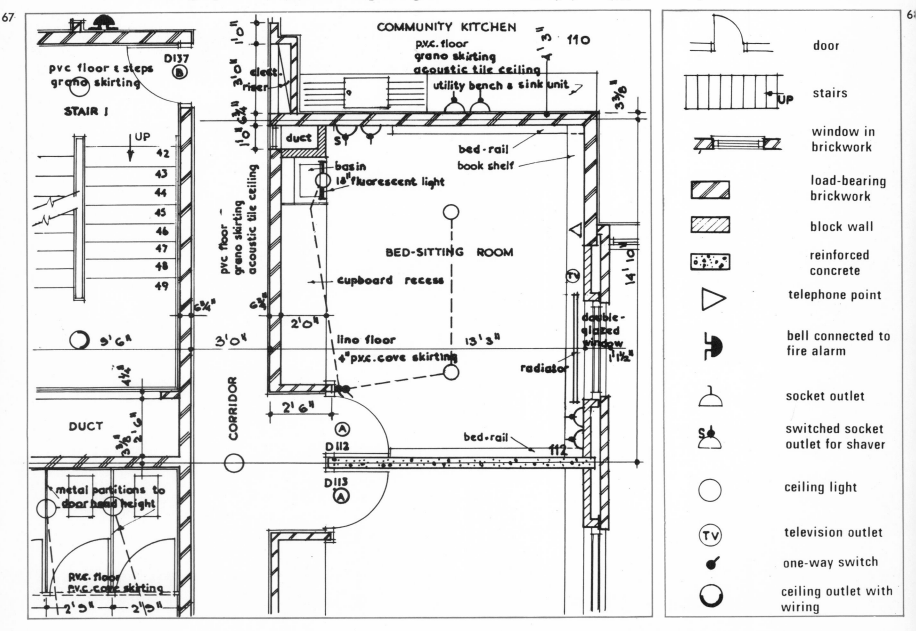

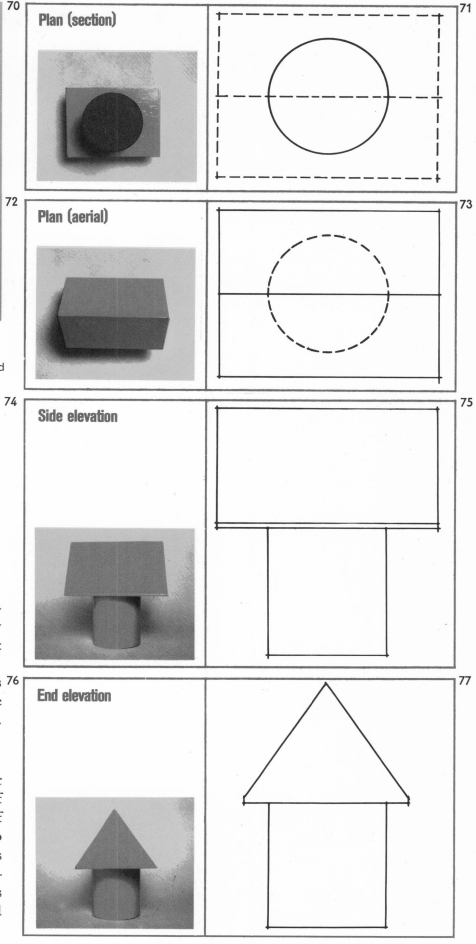

Plan (section)

Plan (aerial)

Side elevation

End elevation

67 and **68.** Architect's drawing and legend. This drawing shows how the architect sets down the information that he wants to be given to all the craftsmen working on his building. As the legend shows, he uses symbols which are understood by them to indicate doors, electrical fittings, types of walling, etc.

69 to **77.** Model and drawings. The series of illustrations on this page illustrate the different ways in which the architect explains the form of his building. A simple model was made and has been photographed from the angles shown on the architects

drawing. Although much more complicated, architect's drawings usually conform to the kind illustrated here.
(70 and 71) Ground plan; shows what is actually on the ground. The dotted line indicates the area covered by whole building.
(72 and 73) Air plan; shows what would be seen from above. Dotted line indicates ground plan.
(74 and 75) Side elevation; shows view from one side.
(76 and 77) End elevation; shows view from one end. These drawings together show enough to enable you to build the model.

Elevations

Elevations show what can be seen from the side. Here is an elevation of the object seen from side (74) (75). Elevations can show the building from any side and illustrations (76) (77) show the object from one end.

You will notice that both plans and elevations have measurements all over them – these are, essential for the builder and even the smallest mistake might make the building impossible to construct.

Sections

Sometimes the architect will want to show what the building or part of the building will look like if it is cut through like a slice of cake. This is a section. You have already seen a section drawing of the Pantheon on page 25. Section drawings are not always easy to understand and are usually read in conjunction with a plan. This means where the section cuts across, the plan is shown. Measurements are indicated on this drawing but sometimes section drawings are made in perspective – usually to explain how something will look. In such cases measurements may not be included.

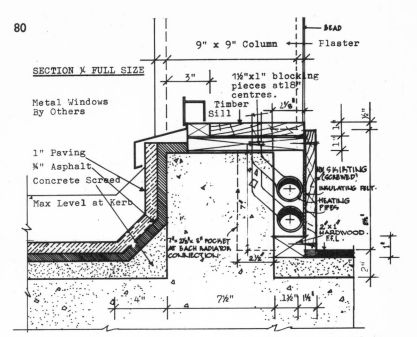

78. Drawing visualising an interior in 1920's.
79. Architect's perspective sketch. This sketch of an imaginary housing scheme shows how the architect presents the idea of his work to his client. It is made to look as attractive as possible.

80. Detail drawing. Sometimes an architect has need to make a special drawing of a part that is complicated and small. In this illustration special instructions are being given about a window fitting.

SECTION ¼ FULL SIZE

Metal Windows By Others

9" x 9" Column
Plaster
BEAD
3"
1½"x1" blocking pieces at 18" centres.
Timber Sill

1" Paving
¾" Asphalt
Concrete Screed
Max Level at Kerb

SKIRTING (SCREWED)
INSULATING FELT.
HEATING PIPES.
2 x 1 HARDWOOD. F.F.L.

7" x 2½"x 8" POCKET AT EACH RADIATOR CONNECTION

4"
7½"
1½" 1½"

Perspectives

This kind of drawing is intended to show what the building would look like from a certain viewpoint. Before the building is put up the architect usually wants to show a number of people, including his client, what he thinks it will look like when finished. A perspective drawing is usually as realistic and attractive as he can make it. Since he is using his imagination, he can picture the building from any point of view, even from the air. Two perspectives, on page 34, one of an interior (78), one from the ground (79).

The illustrations (81), (83) are of the building photographed in (82) and show the use of side elevation and aerial perspective as an explanation of the form which the completed building will take.

Structural detailing

Every building will require detailed drawings of all the smaller parts of the building. These will be used by the craftsmen involved, carpenters or plumbers for instance, to show them exactly how they would make a window frame or fit a hand basin. They are really plans or elevations of small parts. You will see from the example shown on page 34 that they can be very complicated (80).

Diagrams

A number of diagrams will also be necessary to show the general

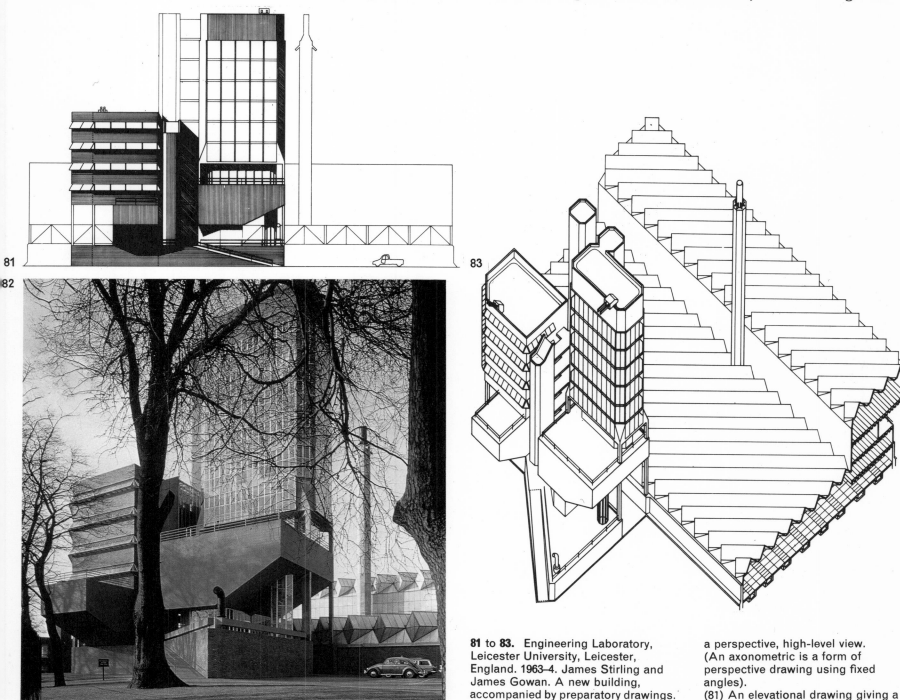

81 to 83. Engineering Laboratory, Leicester University, Leicester, England. 1963–4. James Stirling and James Gowan. A new building, accompanied by preparatory drawings. (83) An axonometric drawing giving a perspective, high-level view. (An axonometric is a form of perspective drawing using fixed angles). (81) An elevational drawing giving a view similar to the photograph (82).

arrangement of certain features of the building, a central heating or air conditioning system, for instance, (32) on page 19.

All these are modern examples, but architects have always made drawings of some kind and here are a few interesting examples from history (84—88). You will see that very often they do not contain as much information as the modern drawings. Building now is a much more complicated process. Sometimes even, the drawings were only an indication and the building was done by what is known as empirical methods – that is by trial and error. Beauvais Cathedral in France, which was begun early in the 13th century, is an example of trial and error method which did not at first succeed. The people had intended that it should be the greatest cathedral with the tallest nave. The first roof that they built collapsed. The next they tried was a little lower. It remained up, with extra buttresses and, later on, with metal rods stretched across to tie the sides together. But they were really too ambitious and the spire collapsed in 1573. The whole building was, in fact, never completed as it was originally intended.

All the drawings that we have looked at are a technical way of expressing what the architect designs. They explain his method of construction. They give the sizes of everything. They show each person who is working on the building how to make his particular part of it and what it should look like. By the time the architect makes these technical drawings he has done all the important design work and should have done all the calculations necessary to make certain that his building will function properly and will not fall down.

We have said something about the construction but we have not discussed the design.

Here again, the architect will probably start with drawings. All the calculations about construction come later. At the beginning he has to think and feel about his building and what it is going to look like and and feel like. The first stage may be a doodle – just a few lines like this drawing (86) by Le Corbusier, a modern architect – or it may be more complicated and detailed like this drawing by a 17th century architect in England, Inigo Jones.

This, for the architect is the beginning of his designing, and what the architect decides at this stage is really most important. It is at this stage that he will make the decision that will, when the building is finished, show whether he was a good, bad, or indifferent architect – or even a great one.

The architect should have, and in most cases will have, enough training to enable him to design a building that will stand up – although newspaper stories about buildings that collapse during or after construction show that he does not always succeed even in this. In early history this could have fatal results for the architect – some laws about this may be found on page 50.

Even so, it is not the ability to make a building that is long-lasting that shows whether an architect is good or bad, but the quality of the feeling that the building has for the people who use it.

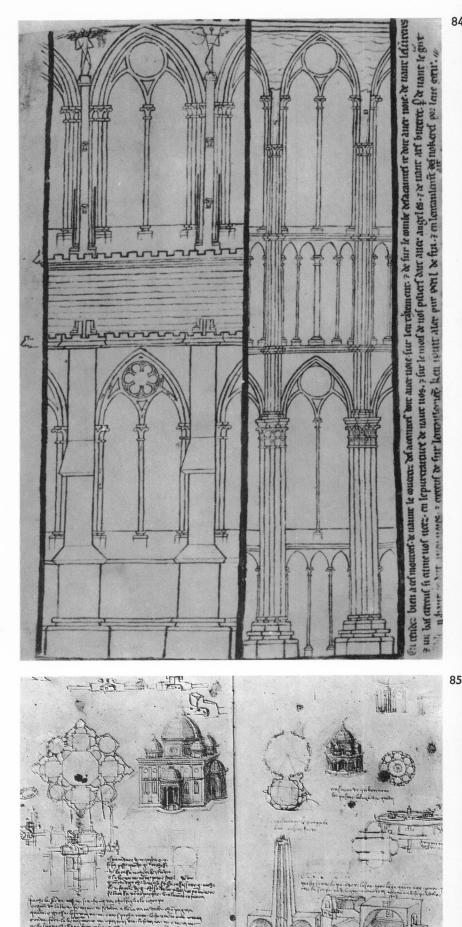

84

85

36

86

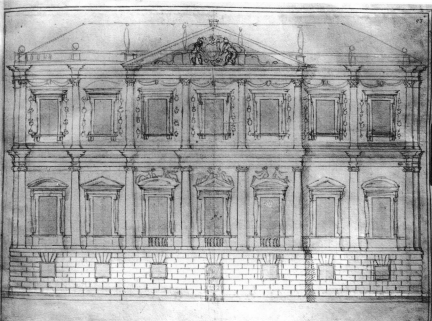

84 to **88.** Architect's sketches. This group of drawings is intended to give an idea of the form of the building as the architect wants it to be. They are all drawn before the building is built. Sometimes these sketches are very quick impressions (Le Corbusier), sometimes they are carefully worked out (Sant'Elia), sometimes to give the architect an idea of what the building might look like designed in different ways (Inigo Jones did a number of different sketches of the Banqueting House). These sketches are always attractive since they directly represent the architect's thoughts
(84) Architect's drawing. 13th century. From notebook of Villard de Honnecourt.
(85) Page of designs. c.1510 from the notebook of Leonardo da Vinci.
(86) Sketch for monument at Chandigargh, India. 1953. Le Corbusier.
(87) Design for Banqueting Hall, Whitehall. Inigo Jones 1618.
(88) Design for a power station. 1914. Sant'Elia.

88

chapter 4 DESIGN

Perhaps the best way that we may begin to consider this difficult subject is with a practical example.

Suppose for the moment that you have been given an area of land – perhaps part of a garden – and told that you may have a house or building put up for you, to your own particular design. You do not have to think about cost, but you do have to decide exactly what you actually want the building to be like. Imagine further, that you have the help of an architect who will tell you how to build and see that the work is carried out satisfactorily.

What would there be left for you to do? Not much, you might think. Nevertheless what you would have to do would be perhaps the most important part; the design would have to be yours.

What is design? Dictionary definitions are perhaps more helpful here than they were with the word 'art'.

'Design' in architecture: 'The arrangement or combination of details of structure', or another, 'A plan or an outline in general for an edifice as represented by the ground plans, elevations, sections and whatever other drawings as may be necessary for the construction.'

All this means that you have to plan all the parts and the whole of the building, you have to decide what shape it will have, what size it will be in fact, everything that will make it the particular building that you want.

In this chapter we shall consider what are perhaps the two most important parts of design, what we will call fitness and aesthetics. To begin with we will continue to examine different aspects of your own imaginary design problem from different viewpoints.

The fitness of your building is its rightness for use. How big or small should it be? What is it to be used for? What sorts of things will be required to fit inside it? What furniture if any? What services? All these are considerations of fitness and correct decisions here will help to make the building exactly right in use. Any mistakes and there will be something not quite right about the design.

But there is still a great deal that comes at least partially under the subject of fitness.

You will have to make decisions about the number of doors and the size that they must be, what sort of handles they will have, what colour and what material, where in the wall they will be placed, which way they will open, whether they will be hinged or slide. When you have finished thinking about doors you may think of windows, or roofs, or floors.

A number of windows are illustrated (91). Which, if any, are suited to the kind of building that you want? The illustration shows the side of a house without windows (90). The dotted lines on the drawing show where the floors are. Of the windows shown which, if any, seem right for this house? The one actually used may be seen on the illustration on page 40 (93).

Fitness is appropriateness, rightness. The choice you made was, presumably, made because you thought the one you chose was the right one.

It might be interesting to examine a bit further how you came to make that choice. It was surely not only on the basis of practicality

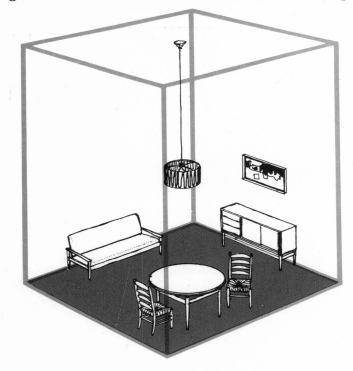

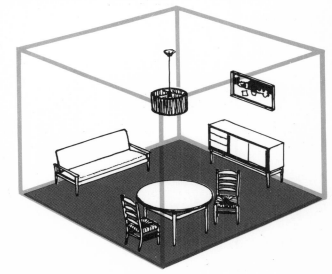

89. Room interiors. Diagrams. These three drawings each contain the same furniture and only the proportions of the room have been altered. In the first two only the room heights are different, in the third the floor area has been enlarged. The effect of each room is very different as the result of these changes.

90. Façade of a house. This façade has been drawn without the windows. One of the windows in the adjacent illustration is correct.

91. Series of windows. These windows are from different periods in history, and, whilst they all serve the purpose of letting light into the interior they each present a different character.

since all the windows will let in about the same amount of light. Your choice must certainly have had something to do with your feeling that the particular window you chose fitted with the building better than any of the others. It must have seemed more in keeping with the rest of the building. How, do you suppose, did you arrive at this conclusion? You made your choice, probably, mainly on the basis of a feeling – perhaps that the shapes of the window and the roof line went together. At all events your choice was not mainly a practical one.

Choice made from feeling and understanding in this way is *aesthetic* choice. It is personal opinion about good and bad, better or worse.

Often there is so little difference between the things from which we need to choose that choice becomes difficult. It may not matter much, but still, in the end, we all do make a choice. We decide to stay in or go out, to buy this or that, to eat this or that, to wear this or that, to watch this film or that, and we have usually some reasons for our preference. The choice we make about whether something is better than something else, may seem to be a simple decision but it is not so easily explained. Such a decision is a matter of opinion and would be described as an 'aesthetic' decision.

Your opinion, although you may not know it, comes from all the things that make you the kind of person that you are. Your experience and your knowledge, the people you have known and their

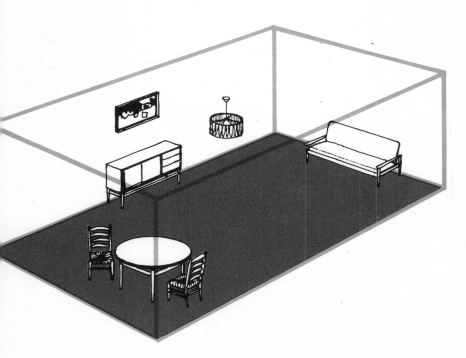

opinions, the ones you trust and the ones you don't, the things you have liked and the things you have disliked in the past, and how closely they are linked to the thing about which you are giving an opinion. This is how an opinion is formed.

This may seem complicated but it is important to have some understanding of it.

Here is an example which may help to illustrate what is meant.

Imagine that you are in a showroom buying a car. You will not buy one with square wheels because even your earliest experiences have taught you that wheels must be round. For the same reason you will not buy one without an engine. But what will make you choose a six cylinder rather than a four or eight cylinder engine? You will know why – or maybe you will not – but if you do your reasons will be based on a knowledge that will give you an advantage in making the right decision for *you*. You will choose, in the same way, the type of car and the make because you know something about types and make. You will choose the colour because you like red or green. Why do you like red or green? You may not know why, but you do know which you like. The fact that cars come in all the sizes, shapes, colours and types that they do shows that a number of different decisions is possible.

In all the decisions and choices that you have made, fitness and aesthetics have been involved. They are bound together by the decision as to whether you choose red or green and which out of the

92. Temple of Love, Petit Trianon, Versailles, France. 1778. Richard Mique. This little building is intended only as a decoration in the gardens of Versailles Palace and as such its design is delicate and impractical. Its form is determined by its use as an elaborate toy. Compare it with the next illustrations.

93. Mauritshuis, The Hague, Holland, 1633. van Campen and Pieter Post. This is the house in illustration 90. The windows used fit the character of the building as none of the others illustrated would have done.

94. Ministry of Marine, Paris. 1757–68. A—J. Gabriel. This building, in contrast to the Temple of Love, has a seriousness of design and imposing façade in keeping with its importance.

variety of reds and greens you choose. It is difficult to analyse why you make your choice, but it is mainly an aesthetic decision.

We have used the word 'aesthetic' several times. It is a very difficult word to define because it is abstract. For all practical purposes we can say very clearly what 'wood' is, for instance, but what is 'ugliness'? Everyone has an idea of ugliness and can say what they think is ugly, but this is not defining ugliness. It only has a meaning in reference to a thing that is thought to be ugly – maybe some insect, for instance. But you may be certain that what *you* think is ugly someone else will consider beautiful. Ugliness is an abstract idea.

'Aesthetic' is an abstract term concerned both with beauty and ugliness.

A dictionary definition of aesthetics is: theory of the beautiful, principles of taste and art.

Aesthetics, then, is a matter of opinion about beauty. That is, about the rightness of the choice you make. It was really this that made you select your window. Of course, we have only considered windows, but it is the same for all the various parts of the building and for the building itself, and for everything else about which we make the same kind of choice, whether one thing *looks* better than another.

The aesthetics of building is how well the architect has made the building look and feel.

What makes the subject a very difficult one is that, as we have already said, everyone has different ideas about this – including the architect. Who is right?

The best answer perhaps is that there is no actual right or wrong. Everyone's idea will be right for him and the kind of person he is.

Of course there are some people who spend a long time considering the design of buildings – and architects are among them – and it is very likely that if they have thought about the question, their ideas about what is good and bad will be very clear. Their opinions will have come from a wider experience and knowledge than those of most people, who have hardly thought about the subject at all. In addition, if they are very sensitive people they will probably be more aware of the differences between one building and another.

We can say that, although there may be no absolute right or wrong, there is certainly good and bad, and there will be some people who will be better able to judge this than others.

When they express their views, they are usually worth listening to, and what they say is worth thinking about.

But even so, in the end, taking into account what anyone has said and what you know, your own idea of what is good and bad is important to you, and it is on this that you will make your decisions.

With architecture, your pleasure comes from looking at a building and trying to understand how it came about, how it was designed, and why it was designed in a particular way and whether it successfully meets your understanding of its own requirements or needs.

chapter 5 BUILDING IN HISTORY

Why do types of buildings change shape and appearance throughout history? Why, for instance, are houses built differently if they are built in the 17th, 18th, 19th or 20th century?

You will already know some of the reasons for the changes. For instance, new methods of construction and materials may enable builders to make buildings that they could not make before. The requirements for buildings also change.

But why do buildings, which apparently have exactly the same use, change their shape and character at different times? And why are places of worship, which are called churches when Christian, and temples, mosques, or synagogues when other religions, so different when they are made at the same time and for the same sort of use? Here are some examples which illustrate what is meant.

This temple (95) and this church (96) were built within a few years of each other. The temple is in India, the Kandariya Mahadevo Temple, Khajuraho. The other is the church of San Miniato in the city of Florence in Italy. They were both built about 1000 A.D.

These two houses were built at different times and in different places (97) (98). Each particular house is very different from the other, although they were designed for one family to use.

Finally, all these churches were built at about the same time in England or in France – with one exception which was built centuries later (99—102). This later building is obvious because it looks so different.

Why do all these differences occur? Why do we have these different 'styles'?

The simple answer is that people are different and live in different places.

Style comes from what people think is right and beautiful, and changes when people's ideas about what is right and beautiful change. We have already said something about this in the chapter on aesthetics.

Style also comes from climate and geography; where you have a heavy rainfall a roof that will carry rain away quickly is essential – like the pitched roof (illustration page 27 no. 53). It is even more important with snow.

Let us look at some buildings whose appearance was largely

95

96

95. Kandariya Mahadevo Temple, Khajuraho, India. c. 1000 A.D. This Indian temple was built at about the same time as the church of San Miniato in Florence (96). Although these two buildings were built at almost exactly the same time and for the same purpose, the architectural character is very different and shows how different must have been the ideas and beliefs of those who built them.

96. The church of San Miniato al Monte, Florence. 1013 A.D. An example of the Romanesque style.

97. Ca d'Oro, Grand Canal, Venice. 15th century. The residence of a rich Venetian merchant, its decorations and proportions are famous.

98. Farnsworth House, Plano, Illinois. 1950. Mies van der Rohe. Both this modern house and the Ca d'Oro have elegance; the earlier in its rich decorative quality and the later in its simplicity.

100. Santa Maria della Salute, Venice. 1631–85. Baldassare Longhena. This church on the Grand Canal is different in character from the other three churches illustrated on this page—a difference of style, not of use.

99, 101 and **102.** Wells Cathedral, England. From 1180 A.D. Lincoln Cathedral, England. 1185–1280 A.D. Chartres Cathedral, France, 1194–1260 A.D. Three churches built at the same time in England and France but which differ greatly in detail.

97

98

99

100

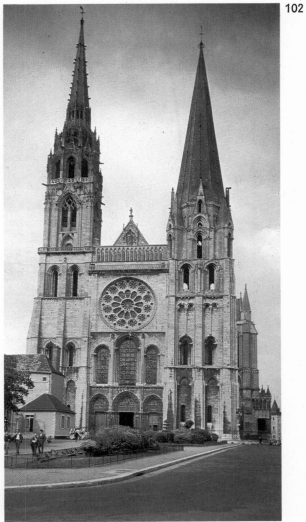
102

101

103

103. Harlech Castle, Harlech, Merioneth, Wales. 1285–90. Sited on a hill, this castle shows how effective such buildings were as places of defence.

104. Castle of Neuschwanstein, Bavaria. Finished in 1881. E. Riedel. Built for Ludwig II of Bavaria, this 19th century Gothic-style castle is in a magnificent setting. Not built for defence, it nevertheless sits in romantic isolation on a minor peak, looking like a fortress.

105. Bodiam Castle, Sussex. 1386. Like Harlech Castle, Bodiam is built for defence and has a similar shape (in this case, square) but it is defended by a moat and is on low ground. This photograph, taken in winter, shows the moat frozen over.

104

10

106

106. Castle at Ferrara, Italy. 14th century. Looking less like a medieval castle, such as Harlech, this building represents the transition from the defensible castle to the defensible palace.

107 and **108.** Church of San Vitale, Ravenna, Italy. 526–36. The octagonal plan, with a dome surmounting the central octagon (see 108), gives a massing of the building upwards towards the roof rather than the strong directional massing of the basilical church of San Apollinare.

109 and **110.** Church of San Apollinare in Classe, near Ravenna, Italy. 534–9. Both the plan and the interior view show the strong directional character of the church. This church, like San Vitale, is famous for its mosaics running in this church above the nave arcade.

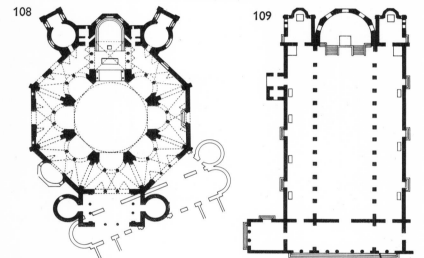

determined by their use. Here are four castles built in the years from 1200 to 1600 A.D. (103—106). During those years, the uses of castles changed. The earliest were great structures for defence and their design was principally a military problem – whether they would keep out attackers, or whether if one part was breeched the rest could be defended. As a result the castle was built in compartments, for retreating lines of defence.

But as we have said, gunpowder changed things and later castles, while still looking something like places of defence, forbidding and powerful, were not by any means impregnable, indeed, they became merely houses.

You can see this from the windows. In the earliest they are mere slits to protect the defenders from arrows and stones, whilst still allowing them to fire arrows themselves. In the later castles, they are large windows for light and cannot be defended.

Here is another example of differences of style which shows that, even at the same time and in the same place, buildings for the same use may be in different styles.

In Italy, in the old city of Ravenna there are two Christian churches built at the beginning of the sixth century A.D. Both buildings were erected on the instructions of the Emperor Justinian. The first, St Appollinare at Classe (109) (110), which was formerly the port for Ravenna, is built in what is known as the Early Christian *basilican style*. The second, St Vitale in Ravenna (107) (108), is built in the Byzantine style. These churches have a great deal in common — for instance, each has some of the finest mosaic decorations in existence — but the plan, construction and feeling of each building is very different. In the next chapter something will be said of the historical differences between Early Christian and Byzantine architecture. Here we shall try to suggest why, in the same place, such strong differences of style may be found.

The style of St Appollinare comes from the Roman law court which was called a basilica. The court was a long hall with a recess at the end in which the judges sat. The building was used by the Romans for purposes other than the administration of justice – for weddings, for instance – and, when the Christians wanted a form for their churches, the fact that the law court had no religious associations with pagan Rome made the basilica attractive to them. Also they had a great respect and admiration for Roman law and replaced the judge's seat with their most revered object, the altar. The long centre part of the church was very suitable for the processional form of worship that they adopted. At the Eastern end of the church a raised platform (known as a *bema*) was placed for the priests, and this usually extended across the whole width, and in later churches projected on either side. This gave a form like a cross on a plan view.

The plan of the other church, St Vitale, is very different. It is octagonal and without any strong direction. The most important feature is the dome and the focus of the church is in the centre of the dome. The visual effect of Byzantine churches on the plan is

111. Church of Santa Sabina, Rome. 438 A.D. This view across the nave of the early-Christian basilica shows how the arcading creates a directional rhythm of arches leading towards the altar.

112. Old church of St Peter's, Rome. c. 400 A.D. Reconstruction drawing. This is an attempt to recreate the appearance of the first St Peter's. It was a large basilica with a narthex (forecourt). The strong directional shape and the beginning of the Latin Cross form can be seen.

113. Capella Palatina, Palermo, Sicily. 1132–40. View into cupola. This small chapel is covered with mosaic which gives a glow and richness that is associated with Byzantine and early-Christian decoration.

usually also a cross, but because there is no strong direction it is a cross of equal arms. Worship inside the Byzantine church did not involve processionals and the altar was placed in one of the arms without a ritual need for it to be in any particular arm.

During the centuries the forms and needs of worship and ritual in the Byzantine church changed little, whereas in the western Early Christian church there was constant change. The result of this is that the Byzantine churches suggest a strong inward reflective character while the Early Christian churches have a strong directional, energetic and active feeling.

Thus, this difference in the churches is perhaps not just the result of someone thinking that a dome would be attractive, or that they just felt that they would put a dome on the building or would rather have a pitched roof. Believing and feeling as they did, either a dome or a pitched roof seemed right to them and suited the needs of their respective churches, which in turn suggests the different character of the two churches.

It is interesting to notice that we have mentioned two cross forms on the plan, one with equal arms and one with unequal. These two crosses are different in character and also illustrate the suggested differences between the two churches.

The Latin cross (114), the one with one long arm, has a strong feeling of movement, it has a direction, it is rather like an arrow or a sword. It seems to be going somewhere. It is active. This seems

to have been the character of the western Christian church at the time and has been ever since (112) (115).

The Byzantine Church on the other hand seems to have been hermetic, that is, it was enclosed within itself. It seems also mystical and confined to unchanging ritual. The plan it adopts, the cross with equal arms, known as the Greek Cross (116) (117), reflects this balanced unchanging quality. It is a self contained cross, balanced and not going anywhere. If anything, the direction is inward to the centre. This perhaps expresses the character of the early Byzantine Church and its successor the Greek Orthodox Church.

These two churches have been discussed at some length. What can be seen from them can be applied to all sorts of different buildings and styles.

The most important point to be made about style, and indeed about all the differences in appearance of buildings, is that it does not just happen, casually, by a sort of accident because someone decides to built in a particular way. Style comes out of beliefs and feelings of rightness, and expresses, usually, a great deal more about the kind of people who did the building than they themselves have realised.

As a result every major change or difference in style comes from an important change or difference in belief and feeling.

In the next section of the book we shall be examining some of the great styles in architecture in an historical sequence.

112

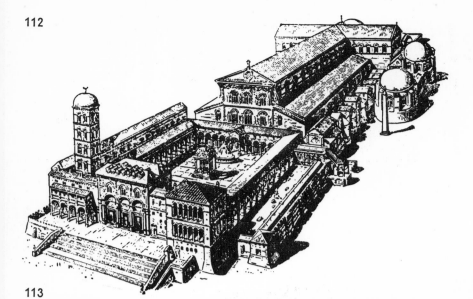

113

114

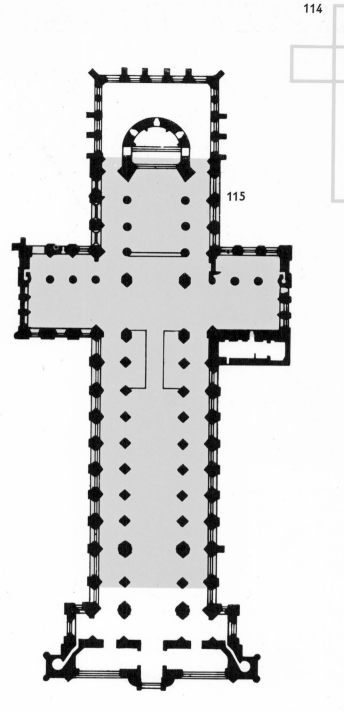

115

116   117

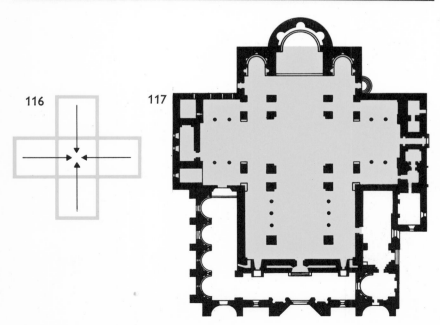

114. Latin Cross. This form provides a strong directional plan.

115. Peterborough Cathedral, Northamptonshire. 1117–1230. A Latin Cross plan of an English medieval church.

116. Greek Cross. This form provides a centralised plan.

117. Plan of the Church of St Mark, Venice. 1042–85. Although the basic Greek Cross has been added to by the addition of a later front (narthex), it is still to be seen in this important church, perhaps the most impressive Byzantine example after St Sophia at Istanbul.

chapter 6 GREAT HISTORICAL STYLES

So far, in this book we have discussed what architecture is. We have seen examples of building in history, we have considered how designers of buildings have made them stand up and what materials they have built with, how the architect puts down his ideas and we have discussed his problems of design. We have also discussed the meaning of style.

Now taking all these things into consideration we shall examine some of the important historical periods into which architecture can be divided.

Precivilised-Buildings

The world's great civilisations have all produced important styles. There was no architecture in the period before these developed – the period when man hunted for food, lived in trees or caves painted pictures of the animals he hunted in those caves and lived in terror of nature, animals and other groups of humans. But the beginnings were there, when men first tried to organise themselves so that they could live in one place and not have to travel around in search of food. When they first tried to keep and breed animals, plant and reap crops, they had to find a way of living in one place throughout the seasons. From caves which they had defended (118), they moved into huts of a kind and began to think about their construction. We have already seen some of their early solutions (page 22). Here are some more (120—123) – trabeation in wood and even simple trusses. The dome shape appears.

This sort of building is like the garden shed we discussed at the beginning. It is not yet architecture.

In certain areas of the world however, men began to develop more advanced civilisations, and it is in these that the first true architecture appears. The history of architecture is short in comparison with the history of man. There are traces of man more than 1 million years old but it is not until about 8,000 years ago that the first true signs of civilisation appear. Architecture starts at about the same time. There are three main areas, one in India, one in China and one in the Near East, Mesopotamia and Egypt. This last is an area known as the Fertile Crescent and its extent is shown on the map.

It includes Sumeria, Chaldea, Assyria, Babylonia and Egypt.

118. Cave dwelling. The entrance to the cave has been protected with logs and brushwood.

119. Fertile Crescent. This map shows the area of the Middle East with the Fertile Crescent indicated. It stretches from Egypt to the Persian Gulf in a broad crescent shape. Here the first civilisations in the Near East developed.

118

119

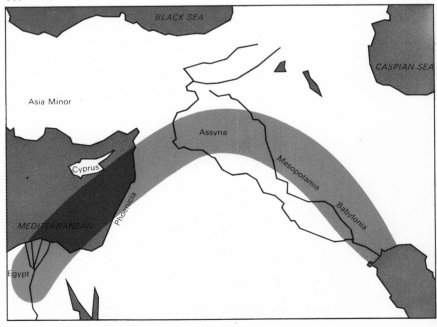

120

122

121

120–122. Simple dwellings. A number of primitive dwellings have already been illustrated. Most were from early history but some primitive types of dwellings are still made, such as these huts and the Eskimo's igloo.

123. Town at Khirokitia, Cyprus. c. 5000 B.C. This reconstruction drawing shows the inside of one of the domed huts—an early form of house, made of sun-dried bricks and with a mud plaster coating.

123

The Near East

The stories of the Old Testament come from this area. Abraham came from Ur of the Chaldees, the Garden of Eden and Mount Ararat, where the ark came to rest, are both here.

The two main original civilisations of this area are in Mesopotamia and Egypt. The buildings that are illustrated here (127—132) are some of the most important from the Mesopotamian area. They are palaces and temples. Most surviving architecture from the very early periods of civilisation are either palaces or temples. The reason for this is obvious; these were the only buildings made to last, the ones to which the resources of the civilisation were devoted. The palaces showed the power of the king and had to be built as strongly and as impressively as possible. All the best available materials were used and all the technical knowledge was employed. Nothing that would enhance the stature of the king was omitted; decoration was lavish in coloured tiles and reliefs.

The temples, too, were lavish. The fear and awe of the gods also demanded the best that could be provided. In early times religion was concerned to a great extent with appeasing the gods who were to be feared, who might destroy the crops and bring famine and sickness if they were displeased. People believed in a number of different gods, each of whom had special responsibilities and powers. Each of them had to be worshipped in a special way and a great deal of time was spent in religious ceremonies and processions. The priests who led the worship were feared almost as much as the gods. It was believed that they were the only ones who could interpret the signs of the gods, and their power often rivalled that of the king. This rivalry between king and priest for power was found in most of these early societies. The dominance of one over the other can often be seen in the architecture of the period.

In the area shown in the map (119), both kingly and priestly societies occurred. Mesopotamia had a strong kingly and secular architecture, Egypt was priest-dominated through most of its long history and religious buildings predominate.

Only temples and palaces have been mentioned and these are certainly the most impressive buildings erected. But of course, houses, shops, stores, stables etc. were also needed. These were, for the most part, made of sundried brick and have not survived to the present (124). Generally they were not very safe structures. It is interesting to note that in the first code of laws that have survived in a written form (the laws of the king Hammurabi about 2,000 B.C.) there occurs the following:

The mason who builds a house which falls down and kills the owner, shall be put to death. If it be the son of the master who is killed, the son of the mason shall be put to death. If it be a slave who has been killed then a slave of the mason shall be killed.

It seems a very harsh law – strictly an eye for an eye – but would not have been included unless such an occurence was fairly frequent. Here is a reconstructed drawing of the sort of house that would have been meant.

The architecture of the Mesopotamian and Egyptian area was structurally simple, mainly trabeational and this illustration shows one of the great palaces. Very little of the actual buildings remain, this is a reconstruction. You can see how the trabeated method gives the effect of a forest of columns.

There are no open spaces in the great palaces and temples of this period. They are made of stone and, as we have said, a stone lintel cannot span large distances. In Assyria the arch shape was used – here is a doorway.

In the last chapter the difference between early Christian and Byzantine plans were discussed. Here are some more plans to be compared. The first two are palaces from Mesopotamia. The other two are temples from Egypt.

They are very different. The palaces are very complicated and confused – or look so at first sight. The temples are simple and have a strong feeling of direction – somewhat like the Early Christian church we examined.

The palace of Sargon, at Khorsabad (127) was built on a platform of sun-dried bricks about 50 ft. above the level of the plain. In Mesopotamia it was usual for important buildings to be built on a

124. Early Egyptian house. This elaborate structure, with its yard, containing grain storage jars, its small slit windows and flat roofs, is the kind of house that was built of sun-dried brick and wooden roof beams.

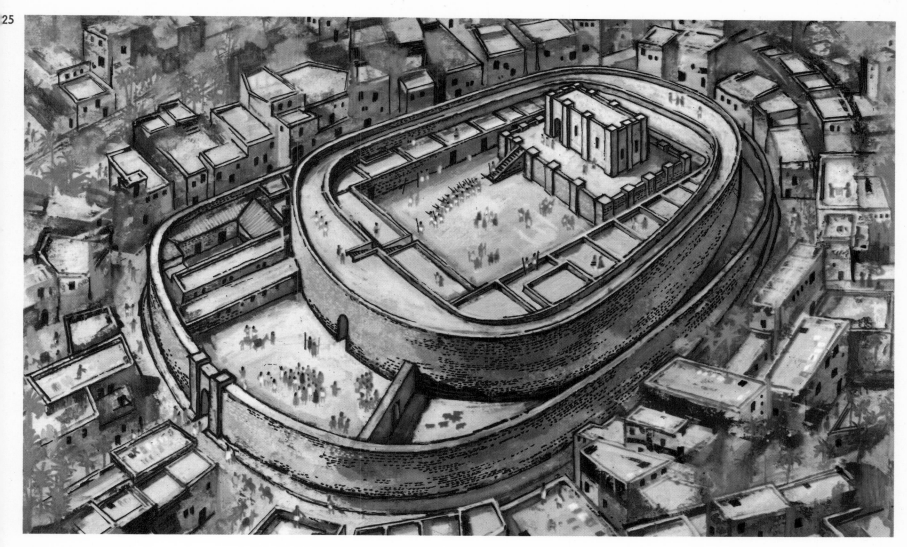

125. Temple complex, Khafaje, Sumeria, Mesopotamia. Third millenium B.C. This oval temple was surmounted by a main shrine which stood on a platform.

126. Bas relief from Nineveh, showing an attack upon the palace. 6th century B.C.

127. Palace of Sargon, Khorsabad, Assyria. 722–705 B.C. This reconstruction perspective drawing shows the main part of the palace on the citadel. The tower in the centre is the ziggurat— the Assyrian temple form.

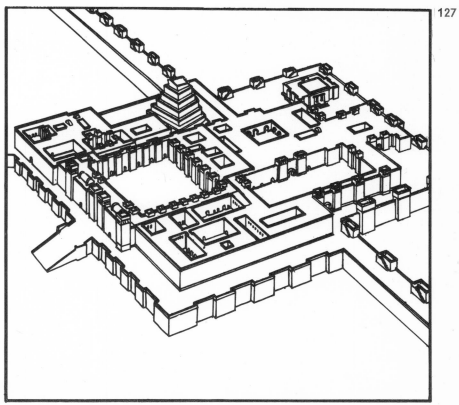

platform, for ritual and ceremonial reasons in the case of temples, and in the case of palaces for impressiveness. A palace is a King's home. It must be large and imposing for that reason. In it will live courtiers, guards, and servants. They will need stores. Horses will need stabling, and cattle and other animals will have to be kept for food. A palace is like a small self-contained city, all designed for the purpose of keeping up appearances – the power and grandeur of the king. One of the usual characteristics of kings and men of power is that they are difficult to get at. They like to be – or have to be – kept from contact with too many people. They are special and must seem rare and precious, awe-inspiring and omnipotent. For these reasons palaces are often complicated, enclosed buildings, with some large apartments and some small rooms. They are impressive from the outside and hermetic inside. The plans show us this – a great number of small rooms around large apartments or open courts, all built on an easily defined platform.

Temples are buildings of a different kind. They are used for worship and in all early societies worship involved two main ingredients, private or public ritual, and ceremonial processionals. In the Egyptian temple plan we can see how these took place. Notice that the entrance doorway, though actually large, seems small on the face of the building when you look at the illustration (131). Also, if you look at the illustration you will see that behind the imposing pylon front, the building reduces in size towards the inner rooms. In Egyptian worship the people were not allowed into the recesses of the temple, only the king and priests being allowed beyond the hypostyle hall. 'Hypostyle' means that the roof was supported by pillars.

Theirs was a mysterious and forbidding religion and the temple expresses this.

Notice, too, how strongly directional the building is. It does not turn around on itself as does the palace, it goes in a straight line through various chambers to the inner recess. The religion was one of strict rites and unvarying processional rituals through centuries. No thought was given as to the meaning of the religion for the Egyptian people. There was only an unquestioning acceptance of its power and effectiveness. Does not the building itself show this? A straight undeviating plan and a building that can only be looked at from the front. The rear of the building has little architectural interest. It is dull to look at.

There is some difference in Mesopotamia. The temple platforms became ziggurats (holy mountains) (132) with an ascending ramp going round the pyramid shape to a ritual platform at the top. In the level countryside this building would have seemed to be a road to Heaven and an impressive landmark – there seems to be an obvious connection with the Tower of Babel in the Bible which was intended to 'reach to Heaven'.

What these temples and palaces can show us is that even in the beginnings of our civilisation when architecture first appeared, buildings had the character of the people that put them up. The differences in the styles of the two civilisations within the Fertile

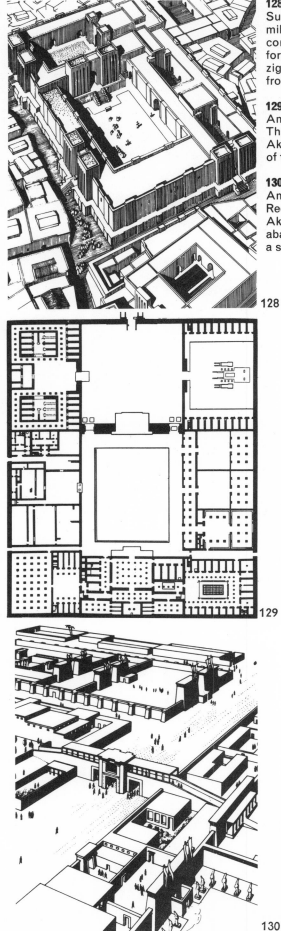

128. Temple complex, Ischali, Sumeria, Mesopotamia. Second millenium B.C. This huge temple contains living accommodation for priest and servant. There is no ziggurat. The temple precinct is fronted by two pylons.

129. Plan of palace at El Amarna, Egypt. 1366–1351 B.C. This palace was built by Akhenaten, the most individual of the Egyptian pharaohs.

130. Central quarter of city, El Amarna, Egypt. 1366–1351 B.C. Reconstruction drawing. Akhenaten's capital city, abandoned on his death, was on a spacious and impressive plan.

128

129

130

131. Temple of Khons, Karnak, Egypt. 1198 B.C. Reconstruction drawing. This drawing shows the processional form of worship of the Egyptians and contrasts with the pyramidal form of the ziggurat.

132. Ziggurat at Ur, Chaldea, Mesopotamia. 2125–2025 B.C. Reconstruction drawing. Made of brick, given a buttress form for strength, this is one of the most impressive of the ziggurats.

Crescent comes out very clearly. The appearance of a building is no accident or chance.

There are one or two other comments to be made on these early societies.

Part of the differences of character in the buildings comes from the different materials used. In Mesopotamia there is little stone or wood except in the north. As a result, bricks were developed and glazed tiles were used for surfacing. These glazed tiles were coloured with permanent decoration. Mesopotamian architecture was very colourful.

Most of the bricks used, particularly in the early period, were sun-dried and were not very resistant to attack, either from human enemies or weather. Even the magnificent city of Babylon, with its famous Hanging Gardens, must have been mainly of sun-dried tile-faced bricks, which have now generally disintegrated and form great mounds of mud.

In Egypt, sun-dried brick was also used for the domestic houses but stone was available for the palaces and temples. A red granite from the south at Aswan was transported down the Nile in huge blocks and this hard stone is responsible for the fact that the enormous Egyptian temples, palaces and tombs have lasted so long. There was little wood, available in that region and therefore stone was used for the lintels.

The external walls of Egyptian temples and palaces slope inwards towards the top as can be seen in illustration 131. There have been a number of suggested explanations for this. One is that they were taken from the old pyramid slope. Another is that since the foundations slope, the direction is carried right through the building; another, that it is the most effective way of combatting the weight of sand which piles up against the building from the frequent sandstorms in the area. Whatever the reason for it, this is one of the characteristics of Egyptian architecture.

Classical Architecture

The simple map of the eastern end of the Mediterranean Sea (134) shows the small island of Crete at the centre as a focus. Whilst the great civilisations of Assyria, Babylon and Egypt were growing in power other civilisations were also developing. For instance, there was the Hittite Empire, in what is now Turkey, and the Phoenicians, who lived on the sea coast in the north-eastern corner of the Mediterranean, traded across the whole of the Mediterranean and went around the coast of Spain and Portugal as far as Britain.

Trade throughout the area was possible because of the sea and all the early peoples used it, setting up colonies or ports along its shores. It was the heart of the international mercantile life of the early civilisations of the Near East and right in the centre was Crete. On Crete a flourishing society grew up (133). It was one of the most attractive of the early societies. Founded sometime before 2,000 B.C., it was destroyed about 1,200 B.C. How this destruction came

about is not clear but the Cretan civilisation was completely obliterated. A great deal about these people is obscure, and one of the fundamental questions not answered satisfactorily is who they were and where they came from. This is important for us because the Cretans had colonies on the mainland of Greece, and in Greece we find the beginnings of the most influential architectural style to come to Europe and subsequently to the whole western world.

The Cretans' most important city on the mainland was Mycenae. We now call the Cretan civilisation Cretan-Mycenaean, because we are not sure whether the Mycenaeans colonised Crete or vice versa.

It is certain, however, that the architectural style of the Cretan-Mycenaean civilisation was responsible for a great part of the formation of Greek architecture.

Greek architecture, together with Roman (which we shall come to later), is known as classical. Throughout the whole of history

133

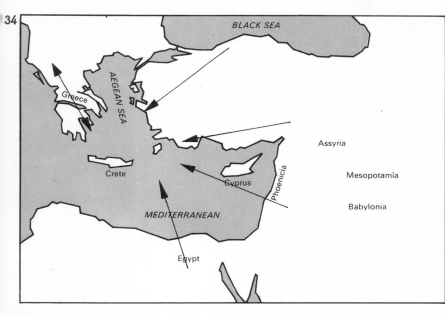

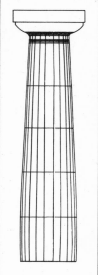

133. Palace at Knossos, Crete. Interior view c. 1800–1600 B.C. Reconstruction drawing. This drawing shows the unusual, shaped columns, narrower at the base than the top, the elaborate decoration and the trabeational construction.

134. Map. Eastern end of Mediterranean. The arrows indicate the general direction of trade and show Crete at a central point in the trade routes.

135. The Doric Order. Temple of Poseidon, Paestum, Southern Italy. c. 460 B.C. The line drawing shows the general form of the Doric column and its pad capital.

136. The Ionic Order. Temple of Nike Apteros, Acropolis, Athens. 5th century B.C. The volute capital and the moulded base are the identifying characteristics of the Ionic Order.

137. The Corinthian Order. Temple of the Olympian Zeus, Athens. c. 174 B.C. The capital, composed of a cluster of foliage, and the long, slender proportions identify the Corinthian Order.

since the time of the great Greek civilisation in 5th century B.C., the idea of classical architecture has been attractive in some parts of the world. So important has it been, that wherever you live in the western world, you will not have to go far to see some example of classical influence. Buildings are still being put up which owe their original form to the Greeks' interpretation of architectural needs.

Classical architecture has been the biggest single influence on building style in Western civilisation. What do we mean by classical?

In classical architecture there was always an idea that all the parts of the building, all the proportions, all the decorations, all the changes in scale, all the materials, should be brought together in a way that related them in harmony. No one part could be out of character, every proportion was designed in relation to every other and the final scale was closely related to these.

This idea that the unity of the building came from a harmony of relationship is the first important principle of classical architecture.

Another important feature is that the Greeks and Romans used the same kinds of forms, seen best in what are called the Orders.

The Orders are the columns and superstructure. There are five Orders. They are Doric (135), Ionic (136), Corinthian (137), Tuscan and Composite. Of these, the Greeks used only the first three and the Romans added the other two. The different character of each of the Greek orders gives each its particular use. Let us look them.

The Doric. You will notice that the column is heavier looking than the others. This is due to its being wider in proportion to its height. It is simpler. The capital (at the top of the column) is a simple cushion pad shape, unlike the Ionic and Corinthian. The column has no base. It stands straight on the platform.

The Ionic. This is more slender and graceful. The capital is curved and has the form, like the horns of a goat, or like a sea shell, which is called a *volute*. It is more elaborate than the Doric.

The Corinthian is more elegant still. The proportion of width to height gives a very tall and slender column.

The Tuscan and the Composite Orders will be discussed later on.

These differences in character between the orders mean that their use affects the feeling and appearance of the building. They have a different aesthetic effect. This use and effect of the orders is another part of the classical influence which has come down to us.

When you come across any building in which the orders are used, whether it was built this year or 2,500 years ago, that building will be part of the history of classical architecture.

Of course, this is not all that is important in Greek architecture. Indeed, we have not talked yet of the important examples except where they have appeared earlier to illustrate some particular point.

Why has Greek architecture been so influential? As a matter of fact, it is not only Greek architecture, but all aspects of Greek life in the 5th century before the birth of Christ that have influenced us.

It is always difficult to decide why things of this kind occur, and the development of Greek civilisation depends upon so many different factors that we will concentrate here only upon the most influential aspects of Greek life.

When, earlier in the book, we considered aesthetics and style, we said that these came out of what we believe to be right or wrong, good or bad, beautiful or ugly. It was the Greeks' ideas about these things that has made them so important – their ideas about the way people *should* live, how they *should* think about the problems of life, how to live together, the laws that *should* be made, what art was or *could* be, what life *meant*, and how people should act.

So much has been written about what they believed, that it is impossible even to describe it at all fully in the space that we have here, but there are two aspects of Greek thought that are most significant for us. The first is that they appear to have believed passionately in knowledge and searched for an explanation of all natural effects. They believed that the logical outcome of learning was doing something constructive. They also believed in perfectability. For them,

138. The Propylaea, Acropolis, Athens. 437–2 B.C. This is the gateway to the Acropolis. The small temple of Nike Apteros can be seen on the upper right. Both Doric and Ionic Orders are used in this building.

139. The Parthenon, Acropolis, Athens. 447–432 B.C. One of the most famous and influential buildings in architecture. It was built in the age of Pericles, the great Greek statesman, and its perfection of proportion and careful attention to detail and siting have inspired architects ever since.

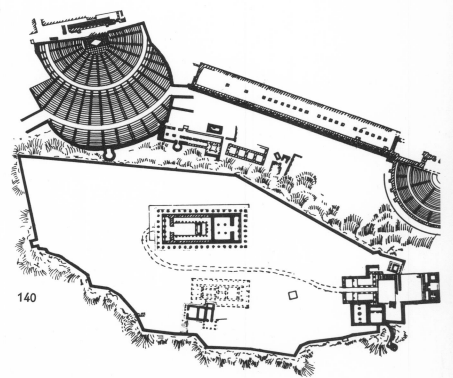

140

141

140 and **141.** The Acropolis, Athens. Model and plan. Like the Parthenon, this sacred site is famous. The model shows how the buildings were grouped at the time of Pericles. The siting of the Parthenon was on an older temple and its position was determined by tradition.

philosophy was the pursuit of perfect wisdom which, in its turn, would lead to perfection.

As a result of all this they investigated so many areas of thought, initiated so many areas of culture, that they have seemed to a number historians to have been responsible for the whole direction of western thought and action.

All this may seem a long way from classical architecture, but, of course, it is really closely associated. In architecture the Greeks tried to achieve perfection of form. They were very careful of the effect of their buildings and went to great trouble to achieve exactly the impression they wished.

Perhaps this can best be illustrated in the most famous of their building complexes that we have already mentioned, the Acropolis at Athens (138—141).

We have said that the Acropolis dominates the city (illustration 140) and that the Parthenon dominates the Acropolis. Let us see how this is done.

The Acropolis had been the sacred site for the temple of Athens from early times and in 447 B.C. a new temple was begun to replace an older unfinished one. This was the Parthenon (139), the temple to the patron goddess of Athens, Athena Parthenos. There are other imposing buildings on the Acropolis and the plan shows the most important. The Acropolis is approached by a pathway that zig-zags up to the Propylaea (138) (the entrance gateway) and passes straight through towards the statue of Athena. Even in all this, there is an

indication of the Greek attitude. As the road comes up the hill, the form and size of the hill can be seen and understood. The entrance leads towards the statue of Athena Parthenos. Immediately one has entered into the sacred area the goddess dominates the scene. The path then veers to the right and, as the goddess is passed, it points towards the corner of the Parthenon, her temple.

You will remember that when we discussed the Egyptian temple we said that their religious rites demanded a frontal architecture and a long avenue of approach which would be impressive. With the Greeks a desire for understanding led them to put their temple at an angle to the path, so that, as it is approached, its size can be realised visually. When you look at any building from an angle you can see two sides and thus you know what the building is like.

The path then runs along the side of the temple to the entrance at the far end (141). Thus as you pass along the whole length you know how big the building is. Again the siting and plan have been designed to increase appreciation.

When you examine the Parthenon itself the same clarity is seen in proportion and detail.

The Parthenon was designed by Ictinus and Callicrates, two architects living at the time of Pericles, the greatest of the Athenian leaders. The sculptor Phidias was responsible for the sculptures.

When they came to build they used the foundations of the uncompleted earlier building. The earliest temples, it is interesting to note, had been directly in line with the entrance.

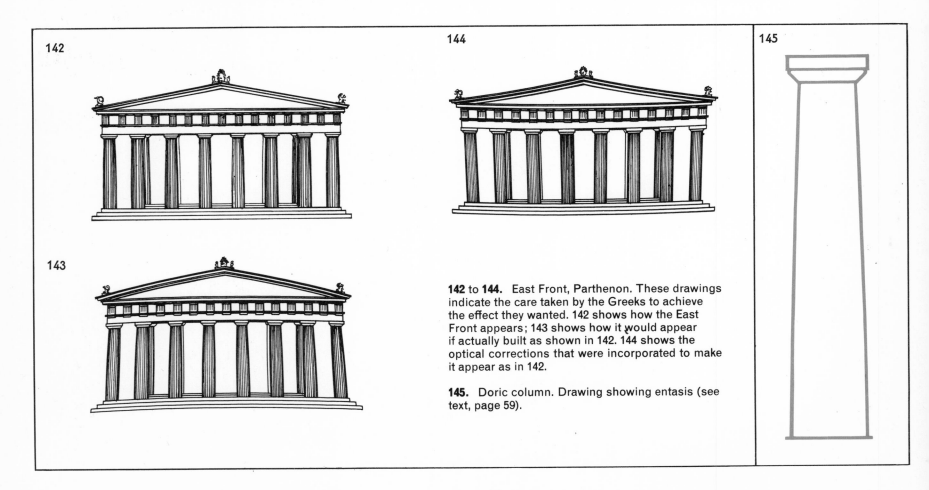

142 to 144. East Front, Parthenon. These drawings indicate the care taken by the Greeks to achieve the effect they wanted. 142 shows how the East Front appears; 143 shows how it would appear if actually built as shown in 142. 144 shows the optical corrections that were incorporated to make it appear as in 142.

145. Doric column. Drawing showing entasis (see text, page 59).

The temple is based on one main proportion. 4 : 9. The use of the column drums of the earlier site meant that the columns had a lower diameter of 6½ ft, and this dictated the whole scale of the building.

'The pteron columns (that is: the outside columns) were spaced 14 ft from axis to axis so as to make the ratio of the intercolumniation to diameter 9 : 4. The same ratio was applied to the width and length of the building (101½ × 228 ft). Hence the pteron comprises 8 by 17 columns in accordance with the rule that the number on the sides should be one more than double that on the ends; the 4 : 9 relation was exactly obtained because the corner intercolumniations are shorter by as much as two feet. The height of the columns equals 5 : 48 times the diameter; it amounts to 34¼ ft, and that of the entablature 10³/4 ft. The two heights combined equalled 3¹/5 intercolumniations and stood in the same ratio of 4 : 9 to the width of the building.'*

This quotation from a book on Greek architecture, even if when written is difficult to follow through, shows how carefully a proportion was worked out in order to give a harmony throughout the whole building.

In addition, the effect the building has on anyone who looks at it has been most subtly contrived. On page 58 are some diagrams which show what is meant.

146. Agora (market place), Assos, Greece. The agora was the general meeting place of the city, the focus of town life.

The east front looks like this (142) because it is built like (144). If built as it looks, it would have appeared like (143).

The reason for this effect is simply explained. Horizontal lines when they stretch in both directions appear to curve away and vertical lines appear to fall outwards – you can test this last point by looking up at a tall building.

Although it is simple, it is subtle. The curve only rises just over 2½ inches and the columns on the outside lean in by the same small amount. It is enough to correct the optical effect.

Look, too, at the columns themselves (145), the sides are not straight. They are curved to counteract another visual effect. When a column has straight sides it appears to narrow in the middle. The curve is known as entasis.

Here is another effect. On buildings inscriptions were carved and these sometimes occupied more than one line. The lower line, being nearer the ground, appeared slightly larger and the Greeks overcame this by slightly enlarging the upper lines by a small increasing proportion each time.

These examples, of course, are only an indication of the Greeks' attitude of mind. They wanted to approach as close to perfection as possible.

As you will have seen from the illustration, Greek architecture is trabeated. The Greeks knew of the arch but, except on one or two isolated occasions, they never used it for their public architecture. This is also perhaps an indication of the Greeks' attitude. There is a

* 'Greek Architecture' by A. W. Lawrence.
Pelican History of Art. Penguin Books.

clarity, a purity about the simple form of placing a beam across two posts. We have already noticed (page 55) how they dealt with the junction of the beam and lintel and the most obvious feature of the orders is the different capital that each uses.

With the arch there is a slow change in direction from the vertical to the horizontal and back again. There is no clarity of opposition. The Greeks appear not to have found this satisfactory.

The Romans were different from the Greeks. They used the arch extensively and also its circular form, the dome.

There were, of course, a number of reasons for their interest in the arch form, but perhaps the reason that interests us most is found in what seems to be the different attitude they had to life. Rome was first a Republic and then an Empire, the greatest in early history, which at one time covered most of Europe (151). To achieve this the Romans had to be an active, aggressive people. Energy and

147

148

149

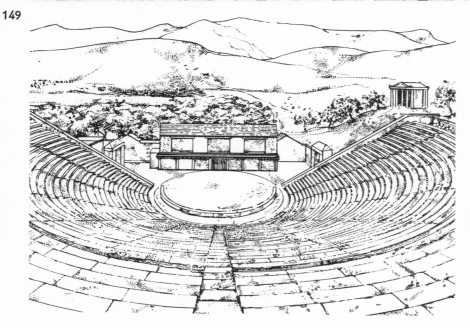

150

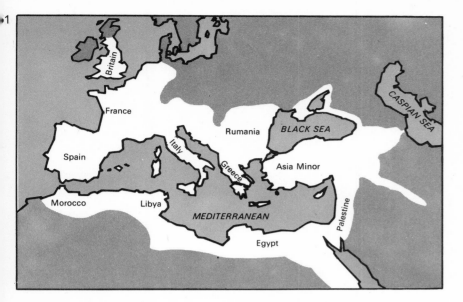

147. Composite Order. Arch of Septimus Severus, Rome. A.D. 203. The Composite order is formed from a combination of the Ionic and Corinthian Orders. The capital (see detail) has both a volute and foliation.

148. The Forum, Rome. This still from a recent film on the Roman Empire is a brilliant reconstruction of the architecture and the atmosphere of the scene as it must have been. A great deal of careful study went into this film set.

149. Classical theatre. Reconstruction drawing. Both the Greeks and the Romans were lovers of the theatre and each town had its theatre, almost always open air. The usual form was a semi-circular sloping ramp on which seats made of stone were built and the stage had an architectural feature as backing.

150. Pont du Gard, Nîmes, Southern France. c. 14 A.D. The Romans built a number of great bridges and aqueducts of which this is the most famous. It has the arcuated form of construction.

151. Map of the Roman Empire at its greatest extent.

152. Tuscan Order. Reconstruction drawing. No examples of this order exist.

enterprise, strength and power, are the characteristics that you would expect to find. Life for the Romans was predominantly active and physical. Generals and leaders of great personality were important, and the personality cult is another characteristic usually found in an active society. Active and aggressive people are only constrained with rules of how to behave, with firm laws but not with careful and subtle refinements. For them the influence of power is more important.

This is perhaps the effect of Roman architecture. They took over Greek architectural forms, particularly the orders, and adapted them to their own different needs.

The arch and the dome are forms that allow the architect to cover open spaces (page 25, illustration 47) (150) – to make big and impressive buildings. The way the Romans lived meant that the monuments, like triumphal arches to successful personalities, the stadia and amphitheatres, in which they watched active, physical contests, are most typical of their attitude to life. The baths of the great emperors are more impressive than the temples.

The Romans in their need for a large number of buildings throughout the Empire were extraordinarily energetic and inventive in their structures. They used brick and concrete, both of which they covered with thin slabs of marble and other rich stones and tiles. This form of covering, a structural material with a more attractive surface material, is known as 'facing'. It has been used throughout history, even by the Greeks. I say *even* by the Greeks, because there is something that is not quite pure in building with one material, and then covering it to make it appear that you have used another material.

The use of brick and concrete and other methods of wall construction such as those shown in the illustrations, all go to establish the Romans' engineering inventiveness. They were great engineers and in their bridges and aqueducts they achieved a standard not reached before. Roman roads still provide the route, and in some cases the foundation, for some of the main roads in Europe today.

In terms of architectural history, perhaps the most important effect of the Romans was the way in which they spread the influence of Greek architecture throughout the western world. If you look at a map of the greatest extent of the Roman Empire (151), you will see that its influence must have been extensive. When it is remembered that Roman architecture derives most of its form from the Greek, you will realise the importance of its influence. It should also be remembered that the Roman Empire saw the rise and spread of Christianity.

The Romans used the Greek orders, and introduced two more themselves. These are the Tuscan and Composite. The Tuscan looks something like the Doric order (152) but has a base and the Composite is a combination of the Ionic and Corinthian (147).

The three Greek and the two Roman are the Classical Orders. They enable you to identify a building as Classical, and are found in all the later architecture influenced by them.

Early Christian and Byzantine

The new religion of Christianity, appearing while the Roman Empire was at its most powerful, spread very quickly and in the 4th century became the accepted religion of the Empire. Of course it did not come about without a great deal of suffering. The early Christians were tortured and killed by the Emperors, or made to fight against each other, or against animals in the great amphitheatres like the Colosseum in Rome. They were forbidden to worship their God under pain of death. During this early period they could not therefore build churches in which to worship – they had to use caves and private houses for secret meetings. Nevertheless, soon after Christ was crucified there were Christian groups throughout the Empire.

Even when the Christians were allowed to worship freely they were too poor in the beginning to build great churches.

It was Emperor Constantine (154) who, in 325, made Christianity the religion of the Empire and who, before he died, himself became a Christian. For political and military reasons he moved his capital from Rome to the old city of Byzantium which was renamed Constantinople.

When the Roman Empire divided, with one capital in Rome and the other in Constantinople, two separate Christian Churches were founded, one centred in Rome and known as the Western or Latin church and the other in Constantinople known as the Eastern or Byzantine church which eventually became the Greek Orthodox church.

We have seen (page 45) how these two churches developed

153. St Sophia, Istanbul 532–7 A.D. This great building is the first use, on a really large scale, of the dome on a square with pendentives. It is one of the great architectural feats of construction. The clustered buttressing can be seen in the illustration.

154. The Emperor Constantine, 272–337 A.D. Through his conversion to Christianity, Christians received freedom of worship and were able to build their first churches.

153

154

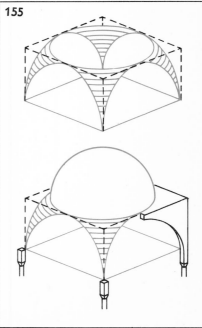

155

different architectural forms. As we said then, the Byzantine church changed very little over a thousand years and its architecture changed very little too. Perhaps it was in Russia where the churches changed most.

The domes are a feature of Byzantine architecture and they are raised on a square plan (155). It is not a simple thing to put a dome on a square – it hangs over either at the corners or in the middle of the sides. The solution which the Byzantines discovered is known as the pendentive.

This is the way that the pendentive works. It is sometimes used with a drum (155). Other early ways were all more or less awkward or unsatisfactory. One of the most common of these solutions was the squinch (156).

In Rome the first Christians had worshipped in secret, but when they were allowed to worship openly they had no buildings, and the old temples of the Empire with their images of the pagan gods were not attractive to them. They wanted a form of building that could be respected. They chose the form of the law court because Roman law was something that they all still admired. This form, known as the basilica, had a long central open space called a nave and on either side, an aisle. This long nave was particularly suitable to the processional form of worship and the altar was placed where the judge's seat had been (158). Thus the Roman tradition was carried into the Christian church. It was from this form of church that the great churches of Europe developed.

155. Pendentive diagrams. The difficulty of placing a dome on a square base resulted in the invention of the pendentive which is a characteristic form in Byzantine architecture. It is a curved triangular form which meets with three others to form a circle. The bottom points of these triangles form a square and the top form a circle. It is thus possible to place a dome on the circle from the square base.

156. Squinch drawing. An early method of providing for a dome on a square base by building an arch across the corners of the square and taking it back to the wall junction.

157. San Vitale, Ravenna. 526–48 A.D. Interior view. The octagonal rotunda provides the base for the dome.

158. Santa Maria Maggiore, Rome. A.D. 432–547. The long nave leading to the altar contrasts with the central plan of the church of San Vitale in the previous illustration.

156

158

Medieval (Gothic)

This period, from about 800 to 1500 A.D., is one of the most extraordinary in the history of building. During this time Christianity became established as the community religion of Europe, and the energy with which the people built their churches throughout all the countries of Europe is almost incredible. It was as if they could not build fast enough – or large enough. Cathedrals, churches, monasteries and other religious houses were built; a community religion such as Christianity needs large places for congregations.

During the 300 years between 1050 and 1350, France alone built 80 cathedrals, 500 large churches and tens of thousands of small parish churches. There was one church or chapel at that time to about every 200 people. In Norwich, an English city of about ten thousand people, there were 50 churches.

All the energy and ability and a great deal of the wealth of the period went into this building. New constructional devices, rich decorations of sculpture and glass were used. The church was the

159

159. Saint Barbara. Drawing by Jan Van Eyck. Early 15th century. This drawing by a famous Flemish artist shows in great detail the actual construction of a cathedral. The great size of the building in the landscape would have made it a focus of attention.

160. Medieval Hall. Reconstruction drawing. This drawing shows the variety of activities carried on in a great hall. The drawing is cut away to show construction.

160

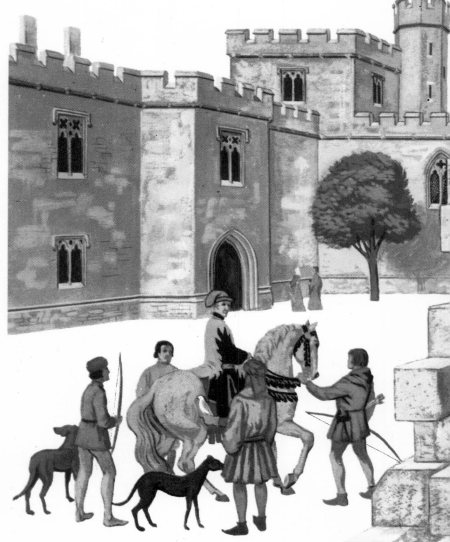

centre of life for the whole community, and all its talent and all the talent it could buy went into making it as important, magnificent and impressive as was possible.

Not only was it the centre for the community but, usually, it was built to accommodate the whole community inside. The cathedral of Amiens in France was large enough to hold the whole population of ten thousand at a service.

The church was the landmark and by far the largest building in every community (159). As time passed and the builders became more experienced, they were able to make the buildings larger and of more adventurous construction. As money became available in greater quantities they were able to introduce more lavish and expensive decorations, carvings and paintings.

It was an age of a new kind of building. The temples of the earlier societies in Egypt, Assyria and Greece were built out of fear of the gods, priests and kings. They were awesome and impressive. The classical temples of Greece and Rome were also representative of a religion that depended on sacrifice and fear.

The churches of the Middle Ages were not only built out of awe and reverence, but also of adoration and love for the Christian religion, which was the centre of everyone's life.

The result of this is that the churches are attractive and welcoming inside. Although they are large they are not frightening. This was a new way of thinking about a religious building.

The form of these churches developed from the basilican plan to the Latin cross plan (167).

161. Capital. Cloisters of Monreale Cathedral, Italy. 1174–1232. The inlay of coloured stones in the column shows the richness that is found in medieval architectural decoration.

162. Royal Portal, Chartres Cathedral, France. c. 1150. This doorway is covered with sculptures and the tympanum (triangle over the doorway) contains the figure of Christ accompanied by the symbols of the four evangelists.

163. Salisbury Cathedral, Wiltshire. 14th century. Detail of spire. This spire, the tallest in England, is a fine example of the decoration of the period.

There are some very interesting differences between classical and Christian architecture. Of course, from what we have said about style, we would expect this. We have said that the shapes and forms of a building come from ideas about what is right and proper. These are, of course, not always clearly thought out by the people who make the buildings. Sometimes they are only felt – and feeling is an important part of understanding.

The churches of the Medieval period (the Middle Ages or Gothic period are other names for the same period) were built in all the small towns and larger cities throughout Europe. We must remember that life at that time was much more isolated than it is now. There were no good roads and travel was dangerous. People preferred, or were obliged, to stay in the community in which they were born. To them, the church was the centre of their lives and the priest their chief adviser in all things – not only religious. Religion was so much the centre of their lives that it absorbed all their energies and care. At this time, when most of the population could not read or write, the teaching of the church depended largely on the spoken word of the priest. Everybody went to the church if they were in trouble, and for ceremonies and for worship. The church, therefore, had to be large and also to give a feeling of protection and permanence. It had to be a building that people could have faith in, could trust. It also had to have the feeling of a place where they could come into the presence of an unseen God, it had to have a spiritual atmosphere.

As time passed the forms of the churches changed – which in itself shows how active the church was. As we have seen from the Byzantines, where there is little change in the forms of worship, there is likely to be little change in the forms of the church. These smaller changes of style within the main style will not be examined separately, but it is important for us to have some idea of the differences throughout the whole period.

Perhaps the changes are best seen in the way the roofing and vaulting problem was tackled.

In the earlier churches the only way that the spanning of the nave could be achieved was with wood or by the use of the old Roman barrel vault. This is, of course, really only a very long arch and, as such, requires very strong supporting walls to prevent it from falling outwards. The walls usually had to be supported on the outside with buttresses. Between them it was possible to put the windows. This was a very heavy and solid form of building and, although it answered the need for permanence, as time passed the builders found more effective ways of supporting the weight and introducing a feeling of lightness into the structure.

Perhaps it may also be suggested, Christianity is an upward looking faith, and the barrel vault does not give this feeling as the roof of a church. As we have said, the arch goes up and comes down again – like a dome, it has a containing shape.

The medieval builders developed a way of vaulting which took the vault up to a point, one of the great achievements of the time. It leads the eye upward and is, therefore, more appropriate for an upward looking faith.

164. Wells Cathedral, Somerset. 14th century. View in cloisters. The effect of the ribs in this fine vaulting is to produce a great, decorative series of compartments.

165. Winchester Cathedral, Hampshire. View into Chapter House. This detail of the vaulting shows how complicated and yet delicate medieval vaulting could be.

166. King's College Chapel, Cambridge. 1446–1515. View of vaulting. Perhaps the finest example of the late English Gothic vaulting, known as fan vaulting from the interlocking shape it makes.

167

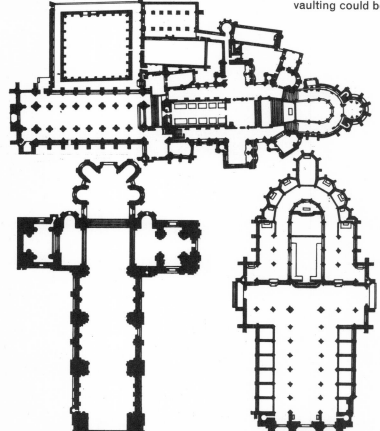

167. Plans of medieval cathedrals. (top) Canterbury, England. (bottom left) Angouleme, France. (bottom right) Amiens, France. In each plan the basic Latin Cross form can be seen, although it is obscured in both Amiens and Canterbury.

This method of construction has already been discussed. One possible feature of this form of vaulting is the flying buttress, which reveals how brilliant the medieval builders were. These are buttresses in which all the unnecessary stone is removed – that is, the stone that is not actually counteracting the tendency of the roof vault to fall inwards and to force the walls outwards. You can see how this works in the drawing.

This method of using a pointed arch in the vault also allowed the use of rectangular vaulting compartments. With the semi-circular barrel vault, the vaults at the crossing of the arms of the cross on the plan had to be the same height and made a square. When the pointed arch appeared, this gave the possibility of varying the angle of the arch to any height, so that two openings of different widths could have a vault of the same overall height. This gave the designers greater freedom and variety in their designs.

It allowed them to make very complicated roof structures. Here are two examples (164) (165).

Before finishing with Churches, we should mention the decoration on and in them. In stained glass, paintings, wood carvings, stone carvings tapestries, medieval artists embellished their churches with picture stories explaining the meaning of Christian religion, symbols of saints and a great variety of other decorations. It is one of the great periods of architectural art and many splendid examples of these medieval artists' work still exist.

Around the church were grouped the houses of the people, small and insignificant. Of simple construction – the cruck house (page

168. Fountains Abbey, Yorkshire. Founded 1135. This aerial view shows the layout of one of the great Cistercian abbeys in England.

169. Palazzo Vecchio, Florence. 1289–1314. A great medieval, fortified palace in the centre of Florence. The watchtower enabled its inhabitants to overlook the whole city.

169

26) is an example of the building of the period. They are not now to be found, as they were usually destroyed at a later time to make way for larger structures or destroyed in war. Of the private non-religious buildings of the time, only the barons' castles remain. But there were other religious buildings like monasteries and abbeys (168) which made religion the centre of important building during this time.

We must, however, say something about castles. These are, in effect, great defensive houses. At a time when the king rarely had a standing army it was the responsibility of the barons to protect the citizens' land where they lived. In return for this protection the citizens supplied his needs – which usually were so considerable as to keep them in permanent want. His home was the castle. This was a great pile of masonry, constructed in such a way as to make it difficult to attack. Its plan was so designed to enable the defenders to overlook and fire upon all parts of the walls. Within the castle there were apartments and living quarters for the lord, his servants and his private army. Frequently, they were surrounded by a moat as an added protection.

Here are some examples (169—172). In terms of construction and architectural invention they are much less interesting and important than the churches.

During the thousand years when the Christian church was establishing itself and the great cathedrals and churches were built, the remains and ruins of Roman architecture in Italy were generally forgotten or ignored. Most of them had been robbed of stone for the early churches, columns and capitals had been taken and recarved for use elsewhere and the remains had gradually become overgrown and lost to view.

The lack of interest in Roman culture is, perhaps, not surprising because the Christian way of life is so very far removed from that of pagan Rome.

170. Walled town of Carcassone, Aude, France. Originally a Roman town, its present fortified walling was built in the 13th century and since then has been much restored.

171. Design for a fortification. Drawing by Francesco di Giorgio (1439–1502). The need to design to cover all directions of attack led to complicated structures like this.

172. Castle under attack. Reconstruction drawing. The position of this castle on a hill prevented the attackers from approaching on all sides.

170

171

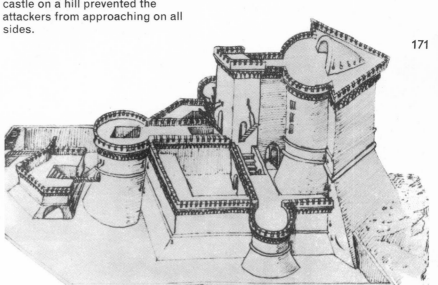

172

Renaissance

During the 14th century in Italy a changed attitude appeared. A new interest in the Roman ruins and the qualities and character of Roman society developed. The classical Roman, and later, the Greek writers, began to be studied. This interest developed into a passionate concentration on all aspects of the classical societies. A new attitude was born. This new attitude is known as the Renaissance – rebirth.

The philosophy of Humanism which resulted lays more emphasis on human capabilities and values than on the spiritual values which dominated the Christian Middle Ages. Humanism emphasises human responsibilities for actions and is interested in human personality but of course Christianity remained the religion of the people.

In art and architecture, the Renaissance had a profound effect. During the 15th century the great churches of the earlier centuries, while they still commanded respect for their enterprising structures, seemed old-fashioned and crude in their forms. This was because classical forms were increasingly admired. Classical ruins were measured and from them standards of proportion were determined which became the rules for building. After the thousand years of Christian building, Classical forms again dominated. This was, incidentally, not only for private building, but also for the new churches that were being built.

One important result of the new interest in individual personality was that artists, writers, painters and architects were known by name for their particular work, and from the Renaissance to the present day architectural development is to be studied through the names of important individual architects. We are not tracing here the historical development of the Renaissance and we cannot discuss all the individual architects, but few are illustrated whose work can give a very good idea of the nature of Renaissance architecture.

Before we consider these, however, we must notice one partial parallel between classical Greece and Renaissance Italy. Both were divided countries composed of separate city states. We have seen how Athens, with a small population, and independent of other states in Greece, founded the classical tradition. Florence, Venice, Mantua, Milan and Rome herself as well as other cities in Italy saw that their situation was somewhat similar to that of ancient Athens and tried to imitate her achievements. A great difference, however, lay in the government of these Italian city states. Although they started as republics during the 13th century, they were mostly subdued by mercenary soldiers or wealthy citizens who turned themselves into dukes and set up their own courts. These courts were the seats of the Renaissance culture, into which came the writers, poets, artists and architects to study and admire the arts of

173

173. Adimari. Wedding Chest. This painting shows something of the court life of the Italian palaces. The richness of dress and the formal courtesy are also well illustrated.

175

174. Church of Santa Maria Novella, Florence. c. 1456 A.D. The façade of this church was added by Alberti to an already existing Gothic church. This is a Reanissance interpretation of the inlay marble treatment seen earlier in San Miniato (illustration 96, page 42). The arched centre doorway recalls the Roman triumphal arch.

175. Lorenzo de Medici (1449–92). Coloured terracotta bust by Verrochio. Lorenzo was perhaps the greatest patron of the artists and writers of Florence. He kept a great court and owned a number of palaces.

176

176. Leon Battista Alberti (1404–72). One of the great, early-Renaissance architects. trained in mathematics and the law, he was interested in music, painting and sculpture. He wrote books on painting, sculpture and architecture.

177. Filippo Brunelleschi (1377–1446). With Alberti, the greatest of the Italian early-Renaissance architects. Interested in perspective and anatomy, he was responsible for some of the first, careful, classical Renaissance buildings.

177

178. Pazzi Chapel, Florence. 1429–46. This building designed by Brunelleschi is a very fine example of the use of classical detail and its façade again recalls the Roman triumphal arch.

classical, Greece and Rome. One result of this passionate interest and study is Renaissance architecture. You might expect from what has been said that the buildings would be careful copies of their originals. This is not so. The Renaissance architect used the details and proportions of classical architecture, but the buildings he required were different in purpose, not temples but churches, not imperial palaces but private palaces. The result is an architecture of careful and respectful but inventive adaptation.

This building is the Pazzi Chapel (178) designed by the first of the important Florentine architects, Brunelleschi (177). It was built as a chapel for a private patron. It does not look like the medieval idea of a church at all – if anything it looks more like a Roman triumphal arch.

This church (174), by Alberti (176), is another example of the Roman arch inspiration. These are early examples.

A later example of a religious classical building, one of the most perfectly designed is this little round chapel (180) (182) which marks the spot upon which, according to tradition, St Peter was

178

crucified. The circle was regarded as the most perfect form, and Bramante, the architect (181), uses it as an expression of the classical idea of perfection. His careful interpretation of a Roman circular temple although only 15 ft in internal diameter was regarded immediately as a masterpiece and it is one of the influential buildings of the Renaissance. It was, for instance, clearly the inspiration of Wren's dome and drum on St Paul's Cathedral (184) late in the 17th century.

Of course, the greatest church of the Renaissance is St Peter's in Rome (183). Here again, a dome was used and the church was originally centrally planned. It was based on the Greek cross which, as we have seen, has its focus at the centre. This form, the dome on a central plan, was perhaps attractive to the Renaissance designer since it enabled him to imply that God and man might meet at the centre of the universe. There are a number of drawings of the plans for churches which are based on human proportions, like this nave church by the architect Francesco di Giorgio (186).

St Peter's was the work of a number of architects through the 16th and 17th centuries. The dome was by Michelangelo (185), the greatest example of the individual genius imposing his ideas on the form of a building. We have already seen that this may lead to very unusual and personal effects as in the Laurentian Library (page 15).

In addition to churches, the Renaissance produced a great revival of private building. The courts of culture of the new dukes and

179. Church of San Lorenzo, Florence. 1420. View along the nave. Filipo Brunelleschi. The classical details of the arcading and the coffered ceiling show Brunelleschi's interest in Roman art.

180 and **182.** The Tempietto, Rome. c. 1503. Donato Bramante. This little chapel is a careful, classical Renaissance building and represents the Roman High Renaissance.

179

180

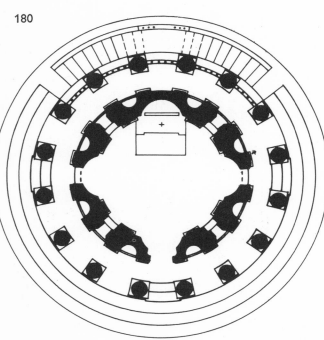

181. Donato Bramante (1444–1514)

182

183. St Peter's, Rome. 1506–1626. This great church is the work of a number of architects, including Bramante, Michelangelo, Maderna and Bernini. Its building covered the period of the Renaissance and into the Baroque. The original Greek Cross plan was Bramante's; the dome was Michelangelo's; the façade was by Maderna in the 17th century, and the piazza and part of the interior was by Bernini also later in the 17th century.

185

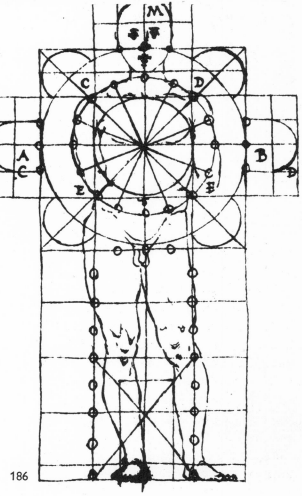

186

84

184. St Paul's Cathedral, London. 1675–1710. Sir Christopher Wren. The dome and drum is inspired by Bramante's Tempietto.

185. Michelangelo (1475–1565).

186. Study of human form in church plan. c. 1482. Drawing by Francesco di Giorgio. This is an illustration in a book by di Giorgio in which he applied the proportions of the human body to architecture.

merchants required palaces. Although there was no possibility of fortified castles in Florence, these palaces had to be defensible, since there was a constant danger from the envy of other wealthy families. The palaces of Florence therefore present a forbidding face to the street, with their main rooms on the inaccessible upper floors, and their open sides on an interior court.

One of the earliest of these, by Alberti, is the Rucellai Palace (187). Notice the heavy cornice running the length of the roof line. This is characteristic of the Renaissance, and is perhaps another indication of a certain attitude to life. Of course, it provides a very strong line to finish the top of the building and helps to make it look imposing. But it does more. It makes a very definite division between earth and sky. It is almost as if the architect and his patron wanted it to be clear that the building was nothing to do with spiritual values, with God or the heavens. Its strong horizontal line runs parallel to the earth, is tied to the earth almost as if the man who inhabits it is concerned with human matters rather than spiritual.

The Renaissance was the time when a scientific understanding of nature and man's place in it was a passion, and the private palace was the place in which such studies might be pursued. The change from vertical to horizontal emphasis is the hallmark of the Renaissance – which, it might be noted, is also that of the classical world.

Whilst the Renaissance attitude to life first developed in Italy, it was soon evident in all the other countries of Europe. Churches, palaces and great houses (188) (190) containing Renaissance characteristics appeared, and the passion for classical learning was expressed in the same attention to classical detail as in the villas of Palladio (189).

Of course, differences occurred resulting from varying local or national conditions of climate or circumstance. We have no space to analyse them here, but it is important to note that, in one form or another, the Renaissance succeeded the Medieval period throughout Europe. In doing so, it gave architecture a new classical look which has lasted into the 20th century.

187. Rucellai Palace, Florence. c. 1446. Alberti. This drawing shows the street façade of a Florentine palace. Its forbidding exterior suggests that it was a defensible house and the main apartments were away from danger on the first floor.

188. Château of Chambord, France. c. 1519. Pierre Nepves. This great house is a mixture of medieval round turrets and Renaissance ideas of a main façade. It has a fantastic roof line.

189. Design for a villa. c. 1560. Engraving after Andrea Palladio. Palladio's designs were used through-out Europe, particularly in England, as the model for country houses.

190. Wollaton Hall, Nottinghamshire. 1580–8. Robert Smythson. Like Chambord, this great house has medieval turrets on the corners, but is covered with Renaissance details.

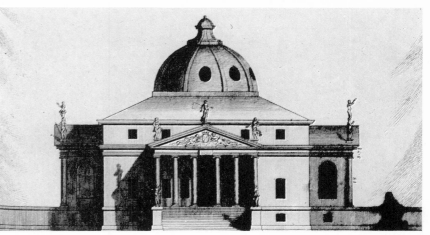

Baroque

Although the Renaissance interest in classical forms lasted until the 20th century, it underwent a number of changes during the time. The first of these changes, better described as an extension of the Renaissance idea, was the style known as Baroque.

Whilst Renaissance classicism was careful and respectful, Baroque classicism was inventive, restless and exploratory. During the Baroque period classical elements, like columns, capitals, domes, porticoes and pediments, were treated with little or no concern for accurate resemblance to their original Greek or Roman sources.

From what has been said so far, we would expect to find reasons for this development in changing ideas of right and wrong, in a different attitude to life. Baroque architecture uses swirling form, and upward moving curves (192). The restlessness and elegance of these forms are found in the late 17th century social conventions of dress and behaviour (193): a 17th century wig had immense curling elaborations; a greeting at this time was accompanied by a deep bow and elaborate hand movement; every aspect of life was elaborate and this elaboration, artificiality, and restlessness, was the result of the tensions and struggles of the late 17th century.

The Christian church, in the 16th century, had encountered difficulties as a result of the Humanist attitude and had become affected to the extent that it became divided. A Protestant church was

191

193

formed and the Roman Catholic church itself was obliged to undertake its own reformation. Reformation and Counter-Reformation within the church, and the resulting differences and tensions between Christians, tended towards an art and architecture which was assertive and aggressive, elaborate and apparently self-confident (194).

The stable but inquisitive order of the Renaissance gave way to the vigorous tense unstable spirit of the Baroque.

The word Baroque has two suggested origins. In Portuguese the word 'barocco' means an imperfect pearl. In medieval philosophical discussion it referred to a flawed argument. In either event it implies imperfection. When the term was used, in the 18th century, it implied imperfect classicism. It was a term of disapproval.

We now do not think of Baroque in this critical sense. It is used, like Gothic (which was also a term of disapproval in the Renaissance), merely as a descriptive term for the art and architecture of the 17th and the 18th centuries.

The difference between this architecture and that of the Renaissance can be seen in some examples. Here is a small Baroque abbey church in Rome, San Carlo alle Quatro Fontane (196), so called because it stands at the junction of two roads, with a fountain at each of the four corners. It was designed by Borromini.

191. San Giorgio Maggiore, Venice. 1565. Andrea Palladio. This view into the dome has the calm, balanced restraint of the Renaissance. Compare it with the Baroque interior in the next illustration.

192. Cabinet de la Pendule, Versailles Palace. 1738. A delicate, elegant example of French Baroque in the form known as Rococo.

193. Masquerade scene in the Pantheon. Detail of an engraving showing the elaborate costume of the Baroque age.

194. St Peter's, Rome. 1606–12. Carlo Maderna. Façade. An impressive example of Baroque design, added to the church and altered the Greek Cross form, obscuring the dome.

195. The Baldacchino, St Peter's, Rome. Gian Lorenzo Bernini. 1624–33. This great bronze canopy over the high altar is in the High Baroque style. The 'barley-sugar' columns twist and turn as if full of suppressed energy.

195

196

197. Hall of Mirrors, Versailles Palace. c. 1680. Designed by J-H. Mansart, paintings by Charles Le Brun. With all the magnificence of its decoration this is one of the great baroque French Classical interiors.

197

198

A curved facade is echoed in the curved plan. These curved lines, like a spring, are full of a nervous tension. They suggest movement to the observer.

In the later Baroque churches, like those in Bavaria and Austria (200), this sense of curving movement becomes a profusion of restless decoration.

Late in the 17th century, at Versailles, Louis XIV converted an earlier royal lodge into the greatest palace in Europe (197). It was the centre of the court life of France and the envy of all.

The design of this palace was Baroque. It set the character of private Baroque architecture in Northern Europe. The plan of the whole complex spreads its paths, like tentacles, in all directions. It sets an order over the whole of the scene – so much so that the great trees themselves are even trimmed like privet hedges to conform to the order.

It is so controlled that it seems to suggest that Louis commanded nature itself and forced it to obey him. This aspect of the Baroque we have not mentioned.

All this sense of struggle, tension, aggressiveness and action, that we have considered is not just a human struggle, it is a struggle with nature itself. The man of power or the noble savage, in either case, was trying to emphasise his importance in the scheme of nature, to put himself at the centre of everything, not as the Renaissance man did, with intellectual justification, but almost as the physical ruler of nature itself. It was an age of arrogant self-confidence. And by imposing this order the French Baroque has a more restrained and 'classical' character.

Since the 17th and 18th centuries were a period of growing wealth in Europe, of colonial expansion and self-conscious fervour, it is not surprising that Baroque architecture, both religious and secular, is found throughout Europe, the Americas, and the colonised East. Here are some examples of the range of emotion and character that is included in the term Baroque (198) (200) (201) and which display its characteristics to the full.

196. Church of San Carlo alle Quattro Fontane, Rome. 1638–41. Façade 1665–67. Francesco Borromini. The plan of this Baroque church is oval. Its façade is curved like a bow, giving the same sense of energy as the 'barley-sugar' column.

198. The Amalienburg, Nymphenburg Palace, Munich, Bavaria. 1734–9. Francois Cuvillies. View of Hall of Mirrors. The lightness and light-heartedness of this room contrasts with the more impressive Hall of Mirrors in Versailles; it is Rococo rather than Baroque.

199. Facade of the church of Santo Domingo, San Christobel de las Casas, Mexico. c. 1700. An example of colonial Baroque in Mexico.

200. Abbey Church, Ottobeuren, Bavaria. 1737–67. Kramer, J. M. Fischer and others. The abbey churches in Bavaria have Baroque interiors which are filled with a great variety of decoration, both painting sculpture, to such an extent that it covers the structure.

201. West front, Cathedral of Santiago de Compostela, Galicia, Spain. 1667–1750. This is a Baroque façade added to a Romanesque cathedral.

Neo-Classical and Romantic

202. Arc de Triomphe de L'Etoile, Paris. 1806–36. J. F. Palgrin. Built for Napoleon, this triumphal arch is an early example of the Neo-Classic interest in the reconstruction of Roman monuments.

203. The storming of the Bastille. The storming of this prison inaugurated the French Revolution, which began the move away from Baroque elaborations.

The French Revolution made a dramatic contribution to the history of Europe. After the execution of Louis XVI, royal heads felt a little less secure on shoulders, displays of wealth and power were more cautious, philosophers and historians looked for precedents for the situation in France and the 'People' realised for the first time something of their potential power (203).

It is not surprising that the display and arrogance of the Baroque faded from the scene to give way to a more sober attitude to life. In France itself, this appeared in a backward look towards classical history, and (because a republic had been established), particularly to Republican Rome. The painters painted subjects from the history of the Republic, and the architects made a serious attempt to produce buildings with all the grandeur and dignity of Rome. This period is called Neo-Classicism and extended far beyond the confines of France.

The first inspiration for this architectural development appeared before the Revolution. In the middle of the 18th century, the beginning of careful excavation of the Roman cities of Pompeii and Herculaneum started a collecting enthusiasm for Roman objects, and architects like Robert Adam went to Italy and made careful drawings which he subsequently used as the basis for design. Before the Revolution an alternative to the Baroque was appearing; the Revolution in making the Baroque unfashionable unconsciously assured the success of Neo-Classicism.

The arrival of Napoleon on the scene as Emperor of France only shifted the emphasis from Republican to Imperial Rome. Napoleon's sweeping conquests, leading to the foundation of a powerful new empire, inspired further imitations of the Classical.

Here are some examples of this careful return to the classical forms (202) (204) (209) (212), more careful in some ways than the Renaissance had been. Such a slavish imitation appeared to some to be pointless and more pretentious than was acceptable. They felt that a more adventurous use of the new materials and a less conventional attitude to design was needed. From this came a Romantic style in opposition to the Neo-Classical.

There was however a very real difference between the Renaissance and Neo-Classic use of classical forms of architecture. The Renaissance architect was inspired by classical architecture into inventive forms of his own, which, although they came from classical sources, were different. The Neo-Classic architect copied the forms and even whole buildings almost slavishly.

The opening up of the eastern trade, the acquaintance with Indian, Chinese and Japanese art, the picturesque quality of the Gothic buildings in Europe, the possibilities of iron and steel, all of these contributed to some of the extraordinary buildings

204. The Madeleine, Paris. 1806–42. Designed by Vignon, this church is a direct imitation of a Roman temple and is in the style known as peripteral octastyle—as is the Parthenon.

205. Newton Cenotaph (drawing). 1784. This design by E-L. Boullée, although never built, is an example of the Romantic extremes of some architects at this time. Romanticism was a development out of, but in opposition, to Classicism.

206. Barriere de la Villette, Paris. 1785–1789. C-N. Ledoux. A series of toll gates around the city of Paris were Ledoux's most important commission and in them he used classical forms in unusual ways.

207

208

207 and **208.** Brighton Pavilion, Sussex. 1815. John Nash. The architect, John Nash (207), turned a small pavilion into an Eastern palace, partly Indian, partly Chinese, partly Islamic. Cast-iron is used structurally in this extraordinary building.

209. U.S. Capitol, Washington. 1851–63. Thomas U. Walter and others. This impressive Neo-Classic building is surmounted by a cast-iron dome.

209

210

210. Fonthill Abbey, near Salisbury, Wiltshire. 1796–1813. James Wyatt. Brighton Pavilion is an exotic Eastern 'folly', Fonthill was a great Gothic 'folly'.

212

1

211. Trinity Church, New York. 1839–46. Richard Upjohn. An example of 19th century, Gothic revival architecture.

212. British Museum, London, Completed 1847. Sir Robert Smirke. An example of Neo-Classic architecture.

which were constructed in the early 19th century. Here are a number of examples.

This is Fonthill Abbey (210), built by James Wyatt for William Beckford as a country residence. It is what is called a folly and only ruins remain today.

Another folly, which still stands in its original form, is Brighton Pavilion (208), designed by John Nash (207) for the Prince Regent. At that time, the most powerful of the revivals of style to compete with the classical was, however, the medieval. For the first time since the Middle Ages, medieval buildings were examined with care and this examination led to a great admiration for the daring technical ability, and the real sense of purpose of the medieval buildings. As a result of this, many new buildings were designed in the medieval style.

Architects and the public took sides in their preference for Classical or Gothic style. Important buildings were erected in both. The British Museum (212), London and St George's Hall, Liverpool, in England, the Capitol (209), Washington, in America, and the Madeleine (204), France, were all in classical style. The Gothic is represented in England by the Houses of Parliament, the Albert Memorial or the facade of St Pancras Station, in America by Trinity Church, New York (211) and in France by the careful restoration work of Viollet le Duc.

Earlier, the possibilities of iron and steel were mentioned, and with the widespread introduction of these materials, the beginnings of modern architecture can be located.

The Modern Period

It is always difficult to know where to begin any survey of a period described as 'modern'. Modern European history is usually considered as starting with the French Revolution. This indicates that 'modern' is not confined to describing the latest developments, but to a more inclusive period which takes in the whole background of the developments important to the present time. The word 'contemporary' is generally used to describe the immediate present.

For our purposes the modern period covers approximately the last 100 years. About 100 years ago, there was a significant development in architecture which was probably responsible for much of the subsequent architectural character.

We have mentioned the use of new materials as one of the factors of 19th century architecture. Since the Renaissance, there had not been any great structural inventiveness until the middle of the 19th century and the introduction of metals, iron and steel. In the first

214

213

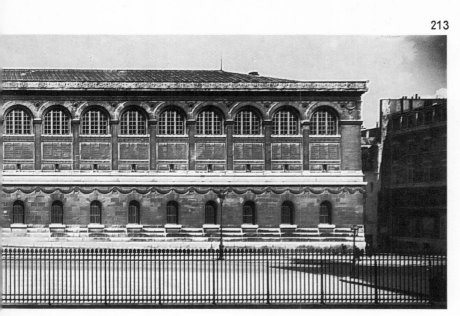

213. Bibliothèque Ste Genevieve, Paris. 1843–50. Henri Labrouste. An iron framework surrounded by stone and given a classical decoration.

214. Paddington Station, London. 1852–4. I. K. Brunel and M. D. Wyatt. An early example of engineering in architecture. The web-like delicacy of the great vault was a new form in building.

215. Pennsylvania Station, New York. 1906–10. McKim, Mead and White. Made of glass and steel and similar to Paddington Station, this is an example of engineering architecture in the early years of the century. Its design is based on the Roman baths of Caracalla.

216. Eiffel Tower, Paris. 1889. Gustave Eiffel. Another example of the engineer designer.

217. Seagram Building, New York. 1956–8. Mies van der Rohe. A steel frame building in which the proportions have been so considered that it has something of the feeling of classical architecture. Mies van der Rohe has been one of the most influential of 20th century architects. The Lever house (224) is an example of his influence.

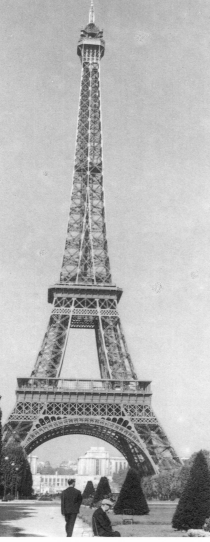

216

instance these were used structurally to meet engineering problems, like covering the passenger areas in railway stations. The growth of the railway system throughout the world during this period is only an example of the great industrial expansion of the period. The great metal vaults of Paddington Station (214) by Brunel, or Pennsylvania Station, New York (215), which has now been demolished, were a new development, which in time led to the invention of new structural methods and materials.

It was this development that inaugurated the modern period in architecture. The use of metal was not confined to railway stations. Labrouste's Librairie Nationale and Librairie St Geneviève (213), and also Gustave Eiffel's Tower (216) are impressive examples of metal structure. In the details of Labrouste's building you will, however, notice a feature that is typical of the time. Although these were new forms of structure, because they were architectural

218. Restaurant at Xochimilco, Mexico. 1958. Felix Candela. This restaurant is an example of the new forms and great freedom of design that the development of reinforced concrete has produced.

219. Monastery of La Tourette, near Lyons, France. 1955–9. Le Corbusier. This modern interpretation in concrete of the monastery is carefully designed to provide an atmosphere of calm and quiet for the monks.

220. Chandigargh, India. 1951–6. Le Corbusier. Detail of roof forms. The sculptural quality of this building illustrates another possibility in concrete construction —it can be moulded to any shape desired.

220

219

221. Guggenheim Museum, New York. Completed 1959. Frank Lloyd Wright. Another example of unusual form in modern architecture. The gallery takes the form of a continuous spiral descending ramp which can be seen on the exterior of the building. This was Frank Lloyd Wright's last major work.

221

in character, architects could not resist the temptation to dress the metal to resemble an architectural style in current fashion. They cast the columns and details with either classical or Gothic features. Labrouste's Librairie is classical with Gothic elements.

From the solely metallic structure developed the combined use of metal and concrete. Reinforced concrete and metal frame construction is characteristic of the modern period. The possibilities of this development are still being explored after the pioneer work of engineers like the Swiss, Robert Maillart, particularly in the work of architects like Candela (218), Nervi, and the Japanese Kenzo Tange (222).

Perhaps the most dramatic visual development from the use of these new materials is that the use of classical or Gothic details has begun to disappear to give place to plain surfaces. The steel frame construction, being a single unit, is not trabeation, and although the idea of classical form as the only acceptable architectural convention was given up by some architects reluctantly, it is now usual to find that the building frame itself provides the standard of division and the decorative elements in the work. One of the more distressing confusions of the first two or three decades of this century was the use of a classical veneer on steel frame structures, because some architects felt that dignity was associated only with classicism.

The ideas underlying what we call classicism and romanticism are apparent in the work of many 20th century architects, but those architects who are looked upon as the leaders of architectural thought and design are those primarily concerned with the needs of our society, and with deciding how these are best met. The classic attitude reflects itself, not in the use of classical details, but in the idea of order and balance and the harmony of the separate parts. The classic-minded architect is concerned, in much the same way as the Greeks, with the perfection of proportion, precision of

222. Olympic Stadium, Tokyo, Japan. 1964. Kenzo Tange. All the work of this important modern architect is unusual and adventurous. Here he has combined a number of materials to great effect. See also interior illustration 233, page 91.

223. Taliesin West, Scottsdale, Arizona. 1938–59. Frank Lloyd Wright. Wright's own winter house, built in the desert to fit in with the bare landscape.

224. Lever House, New York. 1952. Skidmore, Owings and Merrill. This is a fine example of the glass-curtain wall building inspired by the work of Mies van der Rohe (compare with the Seagram Building, Illustration 217, page 85).

building, and accuracy of detailing. He believes that man in the modern environment needs order and balance in his surroundings.

An example of such an architect is Mies van der Rohe. Here are examples of his work (217) and influence (224). There is no added decoration, the way the parts fit together is carefully considered, the proportions seem right and satisfying. It may be described as modern classicism.

The romantic attitude is an interpretation of the architect's feelings. That is, it suggests that the architect should be inventive and exciting, that the possibilities of the new materials, having given the architect a new freedom of form, should be used in unfamiliar ways, to give a visual stimulation of a new kind. The architecture of Le Corbusier (219) (220) or of Frank Lloyd Wright (221) (223) is of this kind.

It is impossible for us to be certain how architectural form will develop. We do not know – although we may guess – how the needs of society will change but it is clear that the kinds of architecture that have been used in the past have gone and cannot return, that the inevitable increase in technical knowledge will provide opportunities not yet thought of, and that there are ideas which are developing now, which may seem outrageous or impracticable, but which will become standard practice in the future.

It is an exciting study, the end of which none of us will live to see.

chapter 7 DECORATION

Throughout this book you have looked at illustrations of buildings. There has been some kind of decoration on or in almost every one of them.

Although we have considered other important aspects of architecture, like proportion and scale, materials and methods of construction, design and style, we have rarely mentioned decoration. But from the fact that it appears in one form or another in all buildings it is obviously a very important part of architecture.

Sometimes the outside of the building may be so covered with decoration that it may be difficult to see how the building has been constructed – look at this Spanish colonial church (225). In other cases the decoration may be very simple—merely the pattern resulting from a way of laying bricks and concrete – as in the Imperial Hotel, Tokyo, by Wright (226).

In either event the decoration is important in creating the character of the building and its visual effect – that is, its aesthetic effect.

Because decoration has not been specially considered earlier in the book it must not be thought to be unimportant. Quite the reverse, it is so important that it has been reserved for final consideration. It is so important that if we are not careful there is a great danger that the decoration will be looked at more than at the structure and decoration may even be confused with architecture.

Decoration of some kind is essential to architecture but never to the detriment of the structure. So far, we have tended to concentrate on structure to the exclusion of decoration – now we must put decoration back in place.

First we must be clear about what we mean by decoration. Decoration is essentially embellishment. It is that part of the building that has been included for its intended pleasurable effect and not for structural reasons. This does not, of course, mean that it may not be built into the structure and become part of the structure, like the sculptures of Chartres (227). It means that the effective use of the building would not be impaired. Indeed the designer of the building is not always responsible for its decoration.

Anything that is done to a building that is not strictly determined by structural demands, and that involves a choice of some kind, is decoration. The shape of the enquiry desk and flight board in the TWA building is an example of a decorative form (228).

This choice brings us back to aesthetics, decoration involves aesthetic decisions. They may be simple, such as the choice of a particular wood because of its colour and texture, or the colour of concrete. They may be complicated and difficult like deciding, for instance, how to design the facade of a church or a palace.

Simple or difficult, the decisions always greatly affect the appearance of the building. So much are we influenced by decoration

226

225. Cathedral façade, Zacatecas, Mexico. 1740–55. Carved from a brownish stone in fantastic ornament over all the surface, this is an extreme example of the Baroque decoration as it is found in Mexico.

226. Imperial Hotel, Tokyo. 1916–22. Frank Lloyd Wright. Detail of window balcony. This building survived the earthquake in 1937 which destroyed most of Tokyo. It is built of concrete slabs and brick and the relationship of these provides the main character of the decoration.

that often the success or failure of a building may seem to depend on its decoration.

We may be so impressed and affected by the stained glass, sculptures and carving of Chartres Cathedral that we may miss the fact that their effect depends on the whole feeling and proportion of the building itself. The glory of Chartres is the relationship between the way the building supports its decoration and is complemented by it.

Having said all this we should try to decide how we can distinguish good and bad decoration.

Here again we are considering aesthetics but from all that we have said about the history of architecture it will be realised that good decoration will effectively express and complement the structure.

Let us look again at the way that this has been done on the capitals in the Parthenon (page 57, illustration 139). You will see that a sort of pad and block have been carved to lead down to the grooves (which are known as flutings). From a strictly structural point this is all unnecessary. But from the way in which the curve of pad has been used to change the direction from the horizontal lintel to the vertical column it is visually very important because it looks satisfying. Actually people have found this particular method of decoration so satisfying that it has been copied ever since.

This is what effective decoration is. Of course, it does not have to take that particular form and there have been other ways of designing a capital.

The capital is a small structural example but of course decoration can be extremely elaborate. Look again at the interior of a church (page 79, illustration 200) built in the 18th century. Here hardly any surface has been left without some form of decoration. There is painting and sculpture, plaster and metalwork in patterns of all kinds. You will notice that where you might expect to find capitals, at the tops of the columns, decoration is at its most profuse. It is almost as if the designers wanted to cover up the sense of construction with a profusion of decoration. The effect of the decoration here is to produce a feeling of energy and restlessness, of movement and richness. This is another possibility with decoration. It may be used to add to or create an emotional atmosphere that the designer wants. It is the same with the stained glass windows in medieval churches. It is also really the same with decorations in an Assyrian palace (232). This is a detail from coloured tile bas relief at the Ishtar Gate Babylon. Bas relief means low relief and these are carved on the surface of the stone so that they read like a picture when the light falls on them. They are meant to be impressive and to induce a sense of awe in people who see them. They create an emotional atmosphere, very like the decorations in a church. The same

89

character of decoration produced on this occasion by mosaic, is found in the University Library, Mexico City (235) constructed in this century.

They are both of a different character however, from the Baroque church and illustrate a principle which is important in decoration. The panels are almost flat and are placed along a wall so that they act as a sort of storytelling wallpaper. They do not protrude from the surface. They do not intrude on the volume, the space of the interior. If you look back at the illustration of the interior of the church you will see that not only does the decoration intrude on the space, it also makes it very difficult to see clearly what the space is. It seems to upset the clarity of the whole interior. Without doubt this was what the designers had in mind and at that time it was felt that decorations could appear to have an almost independent life of its own, independent that is, of the structure. In the Assyrian palace it is subordinate to and dependent on the structure.

Even in decoration attitudes change, and there is no right or wrong. But as we have said, changing tastes bring about different ideas about what is good and bad, and the general taste of today is more in favour of restrained and dependent decoration rather than expansive and independent decoration. At least that was the general taste until a few years ago – now it seems to be changing again and to favour more exuberant forms.

The effect of the restrained attitude on modern architecture is to be seen in most modern buildings. Very few modern buildings have sculpture or painting attached to them. Instead, colour and materials generally convey a pleasant effect by means of their undecorated surfaces. Here are two examples (231) (233). When the architect allows concrete to show the effect of shuttering

229. Block of flats, Marseilles. 1947–52. Le Corbusier. Detail of shuttering at ground level. A deliberate pattern has been made by the placing of the boards of the shuttering in sections at right angles.

230. Cathedral of St Barbara, Kutna Hora, Czechoslovakia. Begun 1388; Vaulting 1489–1558. A fine example of late Gothic vaulting, with coloured roof bosses and an intricate pattern of ribs.

231. Imperial Hotel, Tokyo, 1916–22. Frank Lloyd Wright. Interior view showing the decoration, which used the materials of building rather than applied decoration.

232. Coloured tile relief. Ishtar Gate, Babylon. c. 560 B.C.

233. Olympic Pool, Olympic Stadium, Tokyo. 1964. Kenzo Tange. Interior view of roof construction. Different materials have been used to make strong patterns of colour and texture.

234. Design for a ceiling. Robert Adam (1728–92). The decoration for this ceiling is applied in plaster and comes from Roman decoration of the kind found in Pompeii. It may be contrasted with the ceiling of the Olympic Pool.

235. University Library, Mexico City. 1915–53. Juan O'Gorman and others. This unusual decoration in mosaic applied to the whole of the exterior of the building serves the same purpose as the tile reliefs from Babylon.

leaving a wooden grain, he is using the material for a decorative effect.

In general, then, what may be said about decoration is that it is part of all building, and it may take as many different forms as there are different ideas about good and bad.

A NOTE AT THE END

Building goes on. It has no foreseeable end. We can examine the beginnings of architecture and see something of the changes that it has gone through, or the different forms that it has had throughout the world but we cannot see what it is going to be. As long as there are cities, towns, villages and people, there will be architecture. As long as people have different ideas about the way that they want to live, there will be changes in architecture. We can have some idea about what is likely in the next twenty, fifty or even a hundred years but we cannot know. An invention, a war, a change in world balance – something may very well make our prophecies go wrong. This is the excitement of architecture. Every new building that goes up may possibly be important as a new direction or form of building.

You cannot hide a building. It is there for everyone to see. Everyone can see the growth and changes in the way we live from the buildings around us. It is an exciting and rewarding study. Some of you may wish to become part of it by becoming architects. If you do, it is important always to remember that whether you are designing a small town house or a skyscraper you are not only providing shelter but are also involved in the art of building, the essential practical inspiring art of architecture.

GLOSSARY

ACROPOLIS Most ancient Greek cities were built on hills, the summit being known as the acropolis; here were the principal temples and treasure houses. The most famous acropolis is at Athens.

AISLE Areas in a church usually found running parallel on either side of the nave, separated from it by an arcade.

ANTE-ROOM A room designed to provide an appropriate introduction to a further room beyond.

APSE The circular or angular end of a church or long building, such as a basilica.

ARCADE A row of arches supported on columns.

ARCUATION The method of spanning a space between walls or columns with arches.

BAS-RELIEF A form of decoration which is carved so as to project from the background.

BASILICA Originally a large rectangular hall of justice in Roman times. The form was adopted for the first Christian churches in the West.

BATTER A slight inward slope given to a wall.

BEMA A raised platform for the clergy, found in early Christian basilican churches.

BUTTRESS A large mass of stone or masonry placed against a wall to resist the outward thrust of a vault or arch.

CANTILEVER A beam or girder supported in the middle or along half its length and weighted at one end to carry a proportionate load on the other. In metal frame construction this frequently results in large parts projecting from the main building.

CAPITAL A form used to terminate the top of a column or pilaster.

CLOISTER A covered walk or passage surrounding an open space attached to a church. It is used as a place of seclusion and meditation.

COFFER A sunken panel in a ceiling. It is used to reduce weight or for decoration.

COLONNADE A row of successive columns.

COLUMN A vertical support for a roof or a series of arches. Columns are usually circular in section.

CORBEL A block, usually of stone, which projects from a wall and supports a beam or other structure.

CORNICE The upper, projecting part of a classical or Renaissance entablature.

CORTILE The internal court of a palace or great house.

CRUCK An early form of frame construction, consisting of a roof pole and two simple supports, known as crucks.

CRYPT A lower level, usually partially or entirely below ground, of a building. Generally applied to a church.

ENTABLATURE The part of a classical order which lies between the capitals and the roof.

ENTASIS The swelling outward of the column to counteract the optical effect of the apparent inward curvature of straight lines.

FAÇADE A face of a building, usually the front.

FAN VAULT A system of vaulting resembling a fan shape, used in medieval English architecture in the Perpendicular period.

FLUTE, FLUTING Channels or grooves, carved vertically down the shafts of classical columns.

FLYING BUTTRESS An arch which rests against a wall and carries the thrust of the vaulting from the wall to a detached pier.

FRIEZE Properly, this is the middle part of the classical entablature. However, the term is frequently used to describe any running decorative motif used internally or externally on a building.

GREEK CROSS A cross with four equal arms.

GROIN The ridge formed by the meeting of vaulting sections.

HALF-TIMBER Term used to describe a form of construction which has a timber skeleton filled in by brick or other material. It was used in the Tudor and later periods in English architecture. Its early form is the cruck.

HAMMER-BEAM ROOF A form of roof construction using a cantilever system of wood beams.

HYPOSTYLE Support by columns.

INFILL PANEL The filling between the spaces in a frame construction building, such as a half-timber or steel frame.

INTAGLIO A form of surface decoration in which the subject is hollowed out from the surface.

KEYSTONE A stone, usually larger than its neighbours and sometimes carved, which forms the central locking point of an arch.

KING POST A vertical post extending from the ridge of a roof to the tie beam.

LATIN CROSS A cross with one arm longer than the other three.

LIERNE A short rib in later Gothic architecture, which acts as a connecting piece between main ribs.

LINTEL The horizontal member of the post and lintel construction. It is usually of stone or wood.

MACHICOLATION In a medieval castle, the projecting parapet or tower or rampart from which molten materials (like lead) were poured on to the enemy below.

MASON The term used to describe a builder and generally applied to the medieval period. The person in charge of the construction of, for instance, a cathedral was known as a Master Mason.

METOPE The space between the triglyphs in a classical entablature. It is sometimes sculpted in relief, sometimes left plain.

MODULE A unit of measure used to determine the relative proportions in architecture. In the classical period, this was usually half the width of a column at its base. There is now an attempt among the architects to arrive at a general international module of 10 cms or 4 inches. This would enable the prefabrications of architectural units (windows for instance) to be standardised.

NARTHEX A porch, usually arcaded, forming the entrance to a basilican church and reserved for penitents.

NAVE The central area of the main body of a church. The word comes from the Latin *navis*: a ship – the symbol for the church.

OPEN PLAN A term describing a building whose interior has not been subdivided into rooms for different activities.

ORDER Usually, the base, column and entablature in any architectural style.

PEDIMENT The triangular face of a roof gable. In classical architecture it was formed on the end face of a building by the horizontal line of the lintel and the sloping sides of the roof. It was usually filled with sculptural decoration.

PENDENTIVE A triangular segment of vaulting used to effect a transition to a circle at the angles of a square or polygon in order to form a base for a dome.

PERIPTERAL Columns surrounding a building – e.g. the Parthenon.

PILASTER A form of pillar of square or rectangular section and non-structural in nature, which is attached to a wall and protrudes only slightly from its surface.

PITCH The inclination from the horizontal of an architectural form. Hence the term *pitched roof*.

PORTICO An entrance porch or vestibule, supported on at least one side by columns.

PYLON Ancient Egyptian monumental gateway, usually composed of two masses of masonry with sloping sides.

PYRAMID A geometrical form having a square base and rising to a point. This form was used for Egyptian Royal tombs.

QUOIN A type of corner-stone that is different from the surrounding stones, whether in size, style or texture.

REINFORCED CONCRETE Concrete which has had a material, usually metal rods, cast into it to increase its strength.

RIB A line or projecting stone or wood, usually in a vault, used to strengthen the structure.

RIDGE BEAM Beam running along the top of a pitched roof.

SHUTTERING The form made to contain concrete before it has set into its determined shape.

SQUINCH ARCH An arch built diagonally across the corner of a rectangular space, converting the rectangle into an octagon, so that it can be covered by a dome.

STYLOBATE The base on which a colonnade is built in classical architecture.

TIE BEAM A beam across the base of a pitched roof, holding the two sides together and preventing them from spreading.

TRABEATION The post and lintel form of construction.

TRACERY In medieval church architecture, the decorative carved stonework in a window.

TRANSEPT In a Latin cross plan church, it is the part which crosses the main line of nave and choir.

TRIGLYPH A block with vertical channels, occurring between metopes in the classical Doric entablature.

TRUSS A form of roof construction in which several parts (wooden beams, for example) are fastened together to make a unit of construction.

TYMPANUM An area enclosed within a pediment or within the lintel and arch a of medieval doorway.

VAULT The form of roof construction, made of brick or stone, which is based on the arch rather than on the post and lintel.

VOLUTE A scroll or spiral form used in the capitals of Ionic, Corinthian and Composite orders.

VOUSSOIRS Blocks of stone shaped like blunt wedges, used in the construction of an arch.

ZIGGURAT A religious building in Mesopotamian architecture in the form of a staged tower. The biblical tower of Babel was probably a ziggurat.

INDEX

Abbeys, 68
Acropolis (Athens), 18, 56, 57, 58, 92
Adam, Robert, 80, 90
Albert Memorial (London), 83
Alberti, Leone Battista, 71, 74, 75
American (North & South) Architecture, 11, 13, 14, 19, 21, 29, 31, 43, 79, 82, 83, 85—7, 88, 89, 90
Aqueducts, 61
Arches – see *Arcuation*
Architects, Functions of, 9, 10, 12—26
Architecture, Definition of, 8—11
Arcuation, 21—2, 24, 46, 50, 59, 60, 61, 66, 67, 92
Axonometric Drawing, 35

Baroque Architecture, 76—9, 88, 90
Bas Relief, 89, 92
Basilican style, 44, 45, 65, 92
Beauvais Cathedral (France), 36
Bernini, Giovanni, 73
Blenheim Palace, 18, 19
Borromini, Francesco, 77, 78
Boullée, E.-L., 81
Bramante, Donato, 72
Bricks, 19, 23, 24, 26, 28, 29, 53, 61
Brighton Pavilion, 82, 83
British Museum, 83
Brunel, I. K., 85
Brunelleschi, Filippo, 71, 72
Building, Definition of, 8—11
Buttresses, 22, 24, 25, 53, 66, 67, 92
Byzantine Architecture, 23, 44, 45—6, 47, 62—3, 66

Candela, Felix, 86
Canterbury Cathedral, 31, 67
Cantilevers, 26, 92
Capitals, 56, 66, 76, 89, 92
Capitol, The (Washington), 82, 83
Castles, 20, 44, 68, 69
Cathedrals, 12, 17, 24, 25, 30, 31, 36, 43, 47, 64, 65, 66, 67, 68, 73, 88
Chartres Cathedral (France), 88, 89
Churches, 9, 23, 24, 25, 42, 43, 44, 45—6, 62—3, 64—8, 69, 70, 71—4, 76—7, 78, 79, 81, 83, 89, 90
Classical Architecture, 54—61, 66, 70, 80, 86
Columns, 55, 56, 58, 59, 60, 61, 76, 77, 89, 92
Composite Order, 56, 61
Concrete, 19, 23, 24, 26, 27, 28—9, 31, 61, 86, 88, 91
Concrete, Reinforced, 26, 29, 31, 86
Constantine, Emperor, 62
Corbusier, Le' (Jeanneret, C-E), 9, 10, 11, 36, 37, 86, 87, 90

Corinthian Order, 55, 56, 61
Crete, 54, 55
Cruck Construction, 24, 26, 67—8, 92
Crystal Palace (London), 30
Cuvillies, Francois, 78

da Vinci, Leonardo, 37
Decoration, 88—91
Design, 36, 37—41
Diagrams, 19, 36
Domes – see Domical
Domical, 22—3, 25, 44, 48, 60, 61, 63, 72, 76
Doric Order, 55, 56, 58, 61
Drawings, 32—7
Dutch Architecture, 8, 9, 10, 16, 41

Early Christian Architecture, 62—3
Egyptian Architecture, 20, 21, 23, 26, 50—3, 58, 65
Eiffel, Gustave, 85
Eiffel Tower (Paris), 85
Elevations, 33, 35

Fertile Crescent, 48, 52
Flint, 26, 29
Fonthill Abbey, 80, 83
Frame Construction, 24—6, 27
French Architecture, 9, 11, 14, 16, 36, 41, 43, 66, 67, 69, 75, 77—8, 80—1, 85, 86, 88, 89, 90
Fuller, Buckminster, 19

Gabriel, A.-J., 11, 41
Garnier, Charles, 14
Giorgio, Francesco di, 69, 72, 73
Glass, 24, 30, 31, 64, 67, 87, 89
Goldberg, Bertrand, 31
Gothic Architecture – See Medieval
Gothic Revival (19th cent.), 83
Gowan, James, 35
Greek Architecture, 18, 28, 54—61, 65, 70
Greek Cross, 46, 47, 72, 73, 77, 92

Hypostyle, 21, 23, 52, 92

Imperial Hotel, (Tokyo), 88, 90
Indian Architecture, 17, 37, 42
Ionic Order, 55, 56, 61
Iron, 19, 24, 29, 30, 80, 83, 84
Iron, Cast, 82
Ishtar Gate (Babylon), 89, 91
Italian Architecture, 15, 29, 42, 43, 44, 45, 46, 47, 63, 66, 68, 70—5, 77—8

Jones, Inigo, 36, 37

Kennedy Airport (New York), 88, 89

Labrouste, Henri, 85, 86
Latin Cross, 46, 47, 65, 67, 92
Laurentian Library (Florence), 14, 15, 16, 17, 72
Ledoux, C.-N., 81
Librairie Nationale (Paris), 85

Librairie St Genevieve (Paris), 85
Lincoln Cathedral, 11, 43
Longhena, Baldassare, 43

Madeleine Church (Paris), 81, 83
Maderno, Carlo, 73, 77
Maillart, Robert, 86
'Mannerist' Style, 15
Mansart, J-H., 11, 78
Materials, Types of, 19—20, 24, 26—30, 80, 83, 84—7
McKim, Charles F., 85
Mead, W. R., 85
Medici, Lorenzo de, 71
Medieval (Gothic) Architecture, 17, 20, 24, 30, 64—9, 74, 83
Mesopotamian Architecture, 50—3
Metal, 24, 29—30, 84, 85, 86
Michelangelo, 72, 73
Modern Architecture, 84—7
Mosaic, 90

Nash, John, 82, 83
Neo-Classical Architecture, 80—3
Nepveu, Pierre, 75
Nervi, Pier Luici, 26, 29, 86

O'Gorman, Juan, 90
Open Planning, 16—17
Orders, 55, 56, 58, 61, 92

Paddington Station (London), 85
Palaces, 11, 18, 50, 51, 52, 53, 68, 74, 89, 90
Palgrin, J. F., 80
Palladio, Andrea, 74, 75, 77
Pantheon (Rome), 22—3, 25, 33, 77
Paris Opera, 14, 15, 16, 17
Parliament, Houses of (London), 83
Parthenon (Athens), 56, 57, 58, 81, 89
Paxton, Sir Joseph, 30
Pazzi Chapel (Florence), 71
Pendentive, 63, 92
Pennsylvania Station (New York), 83
Perspective, 34, 35
Pevsner, Nikolaus, 11
Plans, 32, 33
Plastics, 24, 30
Post and Lintel Method – See Trabeation
Primitive Buildings, 22, 48, 49

Reinforced Concrete, 26, 29, 31, 86, 92
Rietveld, Gerrit, 16
Rococo Style, 77, 78
Rohe, Mies Van der, 43, 85, 87
Roman Architecture, 22—3, 24, 25, 28, 29, 30, 54, 60—1, 65, 68
Romanesque Style, 42
Romantic Architecture, 80—3, 86
Rucellai Palace (Florence), 74, 75

Saarinen, Eero, 89
Safdie, Moshe, 29

St Basil's Cathedral (Moscow), 17
St George's Hall (Liverpool), 83
St Pancras Station (London), 83
St Paul's Cathedral (London), 23, 72, 73
St Peter's (Rome), 23, 46, 72, 73, 77
St Sophia (Istanbul), 62
Salisbury Cathedral, 66
San Apollinare Church (Nr Ravenna), 44, 45
San Carlo alle Quatro Fontane Church 77, 78
San Miniato Church (Florence), 42, 71
San Vitale Church (Ravenna), 23, 44, 45—6, 63
Sargon, Palace of (Assyria), 50, 51
Sections, 33
Skidmore, Louis, 87
Smirke, Sir Robert, 83
Smythson Robert, 75
Squinch Arch, 63, 92
Steel, 19, 24, 27, 30, 80, 83, 84, 86
Stirling, James, 35
Stone, 19, 20, 21, 24, 29, 50, 53, 68
Stonehenge, 21, 23
Structural Detailing, 34, 35
Style, 42—7
Styles, Historical, 48—87

Tange, Kenzo, 31, 86, 87, 90
Telford, Thomas, 9
Tempietto, The (Rome), 72, 73
Temples, 17, 42, 50, 51, 52, 53, 58—9
Thrust, 21, 22, 23, 24
Trabeation, 20—1, 22, 23, 24, 48, 50, 55, 59—60, 86, 92
Trinity Church (New York), 83
Truss, 23—4, 25, 26, 48, 92
Tudor Architecture, 11, 24, 27
Tuscan Order, 56, 61

University Library, (Mexico City), 90
Upjohn, Richard, 83

Vanbrugh, Sir John, 19
Vau, Louis le, 11
Vaulted/Vaulting, 22, 24, 25, 66—7, 90, 92
Versailles, Palace of, 11, 41, 77, 78
Vignon, 81
Viollet-le-Duc, Eugène, 83

Wells Cathedral, 67
Westminster Abbey, 12, 17
Westminster Hall (London), 24, 26
White, Stanford, 85
Winchester Cathedral, 67
Windows, 16—17, 38, 39, 45
Winstanley, Henry, 9
Wood, 19, 20, 23—4, 26—7, 66, 88
Wren, Sir Christopher, 73
Wright, Frank Lloyd, 86, 87, 88, 90
Wyatt, James, 80, 83
Wyatt, M. D., 85